SIMPLE BEAUTY

The Shakers in America

WILLIAM C. KETCHUM, JR.

SMITHMARK

This edition published in 1996 by
SMITHMARK Publishers,
a division of U.S. Media Holdings, Inc.,
16 East 32nd Street, New York, NY 10016.

SMITHMARK books are available for bulk purchase for sales promotion and premium use.
For details write or call the manager of special sales,
SMITHMARK Publishers,
16 East 32nd Street, New York, NY 10016; (212) 532–6600.

This book was designed and produced by Todtri Productions Limited
P.O. Box 572, New York, NY 10116–0572
FAX: (212) 279–1241

Printed and bound in Singapore

Library of Congress Catalog Card Number 95–070270
ISBN 0–8317–8171–8

Author: William C. Ketchum, Jr.

Publisher: Robert Tod
Book Designer: Mark Weinberg
Production Coordinator: Heather Weigel
Senior Editor: Edward Douglas
Project Editor: Cynthia Sternau
Associate Editor: Don Kennison
Assistant Editor: Shawna Kimber
Typesetting: Command–O, NYC

PICTURE CREDITS

Richard Bryant/ARCAID 4, 10, 12 (bottom), 37 (top & bottom), 42, 64–65, 68, 116–117, 120–121

Richard Day/Daylight Imagery 6, 7 (right), 33 (top), 36, 46, 52, 66, 74, 75, 77, 78, 80, 87, 94, 95, 98, 100 (left), 102, 114

ESTO Photographics 7(left), 16, 19, 21, 23, 26, 28 (bottom), 29, 30 (bottom), 31, 32, 35, 40–41, 44, 47, 49, 50, 51 (top & bottom), 54 (top & bottom), 58, 59, 60, 61 (left & right), 62, 71, 72–73, 76, 81, 82, 83 (top & bottom), 84, 85, 86, 88, 90, 92, 93, 106, 107, 108, 109 (top & bottom), 110, 126

Hancock Shaker Village
Michael Fredericks 27, 38, 39, 45, 63, 91, 104–105, 112–113, 115, 118
Paul Rocheleau 14 bottom, 67, 89, 96–97

Buddy Mays/Travel Stock 17, 22, 33 (bottom), 48, 127

Paul Myers 14 (top), 30 (top)

New England Stock Photo
J. Christopher 111
Jean Higgins 24–25
Jim Schwabel 34, 55, 69 (top & bottom), 103 (bottom)

North Wind Picture Archives 5, 11, 12 (top), 13

Western Reserve Historical Society 122, 123, 124, 125

Woodfin Camp & Associates
Sam Abell 15, 70
Bill Strode 18
Chris Tortora 103 (top)

Unicorn Stock Photos
Robert W. Ginn 56–57
Jeff Greenberg 116 (left)
Jean Higgins 8–9, 43, 99, 100–101
D & I MacDonald 53, 79, 119
Paul Murphy 20
Chris Schmeiser 28 (top)

CONTENTS

INTRODUCTION

The Shakers, during the time of their ascendancy only one of numerous millennial groups active in the United States, have become in the past twenty years the center of a cult of artistic appreciation expressing itself in books, symposia, and six-figure auction prices. Ironically, all this recent attention to the United Society of Believers in Christ's First and Second Appearing, as they called themselves, is for a group of humble people who sought only to remove themselves from the world's cares and perceived vices. As separatists, the Shakers were a unit of extreme religious enthusiasts. However, unlike contemporary groups, they created a body of art and craft that will long survive their religious works.

SHAKER HISTORY

The history of the Shakers began in France with a few Protestants known as Camisards. Persecuted by the ruling Catholics both for their heretical views and their religious practices, which involved trancelike states and violently agitated expressions of faith, they fled to England in 1706. There they found new adherents among disaffected Quakers, Anglicans, and Methodists, and forged a religious community referred to as the "Shaking Quakers"—a reference to the exuberance of its ritual expression.

One of the new English believers was a poverty-stricken young Manchester woman named Ann Lee (1736–1784), who had lost four children in infancy by the time she was thirty and had, perhaps not surprisingly, developed a distaste for both sex and procreation. Ann was subject to what she perceived as religious visions, and her sharp memory of these occurrences combined with powerful oratorical skills soon elevated her to a position of power within the fledgling religious organization. They attracted the attention of the English authorities, and Ann Lee was imprisoned in 1770 for preaching heresy, including what even today would be regarded as heretical by most organized religion: the belief in a deity with dual male and female aspects.

BELOW: Illustration from a nineteenth-century book dealing with Shaker life. Group singing and dancing were an important aspect of Shaker religious expression.

LEFT: In this room at Hancock Shaker Village, Massachusetts, a slant-lid desk box is set on a table to provide a simple desk. In the background is a built-in cupboard and drawers.

Stoned and ridiculed in England, she and her few followers fled in 1774 to the New World colonies, where after two years in New York City, they established a community at Niskeyuna (later Watervliet), New York, west of Albany. Filled with holy enthusiasm and capitalizing on the religious ferment of the times, the Shakers spread their faith through New England and west, establishing one community after another—Mount [New] Lebanon, Sodus, and Groveland, New York; Hancock and Harvard, Massachusetts; Enfield, Connecticut; Canterbury and Enfield, New Hampshire; Alfred and Sabbathday Lake, Maine; Pleasant Hill and South Union, Kentucky; and Union Village and North Union, Ohio.

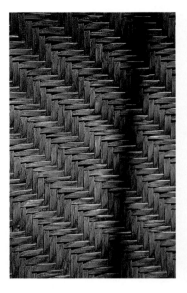

ABOVE: Detail of the woven splint seat of a nineteenth-century side chair from South Union, Kentucky, showing the great care in weaving typical of community craftsmen.

LEFT: Oval boxes, c. 1880–1920; maple with pine top and bottom, lapped construction, New York or New England. These storage boxes were made in graduated sizes or "nests."

FOLLOWING PAGE: View of the landscape around the Canterbury Shaker Village, New Hampshire. Established in 1792, the Canterbury Community remained active until 1990, producing a wide variety of furniture and accessories.

LEFT: Chest or "case" or drawers in cherry, c. 1830–1850; Kentucky. The sides are paneled rather than made from solid blocks of wood.

By the 1850s, between four to five thousand people had converted to the Shaker faith and had settled in the highly structured communities. Though Mother Ann Lee, as their first strong leader came to be known, died in 1784, she was succeeded by other leaders who preached her virtues: faith, hope, honesty, continence, conscience, simplicity, meekness, humility, prudence, patience, thankfulness, and charity.

Many of these goals differed little from those advocated by other religious groups. However, certain of them created inevitable conflicts with surrounding communities. Total celibacy and a revolutionary belief in racial and sexual equality clashed both with general belief and secular law. Additionally, communal property holding gave the group advantages in the commercial world that were both evident and resented. Shaker pacifism also rankled those who were sending sons to die in the Mexican, Civil, and Spanish-American Wars.

However, the Shakers were generally respected for their honesty in business dealings and for the services they provided. They gave generously to the poor, and their grammar schools were often open to non-Shaker children. They frequently refused to patent their many inventions and improvements on existing technology, and they introduced patent medicines and garden seeds which benefited the world in general.

BELOW: Community at Canterbury, New Hampshire, as depicted in a book of the period. Shaker communities were really small, self-contained villages.

Yet they were also quite unfashionable. Mother Ann had preached against any show of wealth or finery, and those who followed her in command put into practice the dictum that form should follow function. In their theological treatise, *A Summary View of the Millennial Church or United Society of Believers*, published in 1823, the Elders Calvin Green and Seth Youngs Wells noted that "Any thing may, with strict propriety, be called perfect, which perfectly answers the purpose for which it was designed."

In practice this led to the development of furniture, household accessories, tools, and clothing which in their simplicity and lack of decoration stood in sharp contrast to many similar objects being produced in the "World," as Shakers referred to the society of non-Believers. This sparse design and unencumbered line, so outré in its day, seems eye-catchingly modern in ours. As a result, Shaker-made products, from chairs and tables to cloaks and bonnets, have become highly collectible both in America and abroad where, in Scandinavia, Shaker workmanship has had a direct influence on contemporary design.

LEFT: Interior of the great round barn at Hancock Shaker Village, Massachusetts. The Shakers were highly innovative in their farming methods. This barn was devised to provide more efficiently for the care of cattle.

As for the Shakers themselves, they have by now seriously dwindled. Religious enthusiasm waned after the Civil War; also the development of orphanages and County Homes offered an alternative for the widows and children who had always been a source of converts to Shakerism. Industrialization and the opening of more fertile western farm lands gradually eliminated the advantages in growth and production that communality and native ingenuity had given the Shakers.

By the early 1900s, most of the western communities had too few members to continue. Their lands were sold, and the remaining believers fell back on the eastern bastions. Watervliet, New York, the seminal settlement, closed in 1938, followed by Mount Lebanon in 1947. By this time the New Hampshire colonies were gone as well, and the

ABOVE: A group of Shaker Brothers and Sisters on a sleigh ride. Contrary to popular belief, the Shakers did not spend all their time at work and in prayer, but on occasion indulged in various sports and outdoor activities.

Hancock, Massachusetts, Community closed in 1959–1960. Today, only the small Family at Sabbathday Lake, Maine, remains. But Shaker art and craft remain as a precious and vital contribution to American cultural life.

THE CITY OF LIGHT: SHAKER ARCHITECTURE

Shakerism was a faith that wholly encompassed its adherents' lives. Architecture, living arrangements, work, and social customs were designed to further the purposes of the holy "empire on earth," since it was thought that the faithful were in union with God, and therefore actually living in a sort of terrestrial heaven. In furtherance of this hierarchical design, communities were divided into seven units termed bishoprics, each of which consisted of several closely related villages. Governing the bishoprics were ministries made up of four Elders, two men and two women of equal voice.

RIGHT: Round cut-stone and wood barn at Hancock Shaker Village, Massachusetts. Part of the Church Family complex, this barn was hailed as an important nineteenth-century innovation in the dairy industry.

The authority of the Elders was eventually embodied in the so-called Millennial Laws, which dictated in minute detail not only the religious but also the temporal life of the Believers. There were not only rules governing time and method of worship but also detailed regulations covering daily conduct, dress, travel, contact with non-Believers, and even such minutiae as the size of mirrors (those larger than 12 by 18 inches "ought never to be purchased by Believers") and the color of beds (green was the primary choice).

Shaker architecture and design reflected the sect's fundamental beliefs. Since celibacy was mandated and humans tend

ABOVE: Illustration from a nineteenth-century book depicting Shakers taking part in a religious dance or "exercise." Worldly people were fascinated with Shaker life, and often attended these devotions much as they would a sporting event.

to stray, elaborate precautions were taken to separate the sexes. Villages were divided into units often given geographical designations such as "North" or "South" Family; and within these units the structures customarily had two entrances, one for men, the other for women. Separate sleeping quarters, or "retiring rooms," had single-sex stairways (usually, men on the left of the house, women on the right) and meals were taken in a segregated dining room.

Work was divided along more or less traditional lines, with women responsible for the cleaning, sewing, washing, cooking, and caring for girls (who were housed in their own unit; men cared for the boys separately), while men toiled in the shops and fields or traveled forth on worldly business. Other than a weekly "social hour"(Union Meetings) men and women came together primarily during the course of religious observances, which featured singing and dancing of such intensity and fervor that in later years large numbers of non-Shakers came to watch and marvel.

RELIGION AND DESIGN

While it is true that Shaker architecture mirrored their beliefs, it also reflected contemporary design to the extent that few visitors to a community would find it unfamiliar. The earliest buildings were of clapboard or stone in the Federal or Georgian manner, lacking, of course, decorative embellishments such as pillars or Paladian windows. Brick followed, and in the later, western communities Empire and Victorian masses and details intruded upon the severe lines inherited from the eighteenth century.

Both inside and out, Shaker structures reflected the strictures of religious doctrines which dictated that "beadings, mouldings, and cornices which are merely for fancy may not be made by Believers. Odd or fanciful styles of architecture may not be used among Believers, neither should any deviate widely from the common styles of buildings among Believers." Wooden exteriors were purposefully painted—the central meeting house was white and other buildings yellow or red. Plastered interiors were universally white with woodwork usually painted, according to Millennial Law, a dark blue-green and floors left unfinished or stained a yellow-ochre.

ABOVE: Interior of a meeting-house. The congregation sat on the benches arranged about the walls while the central floor remained clear for the ritual dancing that was a part of Shaker devotions.

Such limitations actually worked to the Shakers' advantage in that not only was money saved through avoidance of costly architectural embellishments, but also such uniformity in design allowed for substantial savings in material and construction costs. Moreover, out of this doctrine evolved a pared down version of classical architecture (popular in this country c. 1780–1840), which in its simplicity of line and mass is immediately appealing to the contemporary eye.

Shaker conservatism extended only to those architectural elements which they regarded as "superfluous." In all other respects they sought out and adopted the most modern technology. At a time when many in New England were heating with fireplaces, the Shakers installed efficient stoves of their own design and manufacture, including bake ovens with a novel arrangement of dampers for heat control. They eliminated the need for treks to the privy, or outhouse, by producing vented interior close seats or "necessaries," and their workrooms, kitchens, and laundries were filled with labor-saving devices. Often they were among the first in an area to take advantage of modern conveniences like electricity.

Shaker furnishings were designed to relate efficiently to the space in which they were to be placed, with a fine balance between comfort and practicality. Thus the Laws of 1845 prescribed for each "retiring room" a rocking chair ("except where the aged reside"), a table, one or two

LEFT: Shaker architecture and design reflected the sect's fundamental belief in celibacy. This view shows a typical segregated dining hall, where men and women took their meals sitting at tables on opposite sides of the room.

RIGHT: Arched doorway looking into the dining area of a building at Shakertown, Pleasant Hill, Kentucky. Note the fan light and finely paneled single door.

lamp stands, and a looking-glass of the allowed size. Since Believers were expected to spend little time other than sleeping in these rooms this was deemed sufficient.

An important element of interior design was the pegboard which ran about the upper walls of most rooms. Chairs and other furnishings could be hung upon them, allowing the rooms to be more readily cleaned. Moreover, set against the stark white walls, the narrow boards served as interesting details.

Constant concern for the relationship between furnishings and the space they occupied was shown in the community areas of the villages. The meeting houses were furnished with benches, which could be moved and stacked to allow for the ritual dances that were an important part of the group's theology. A wooden wainscoting, usually stained dark brown, ran about the lower portion of the walls thus preventing damage to the fragile plaster, while the cast-iron stoves were mounted on slate or fieldstone platforms to reduce the risk of fire.

In no area of domestic architecture were the Shakers more creative than in that of storage units. At a time where few worldly homes had closets (relying instead on large armoires or Kasten), they devised a complex system of built-in storage spaces as an integral part of building interiors. Sets of drawers, cupboards, cupboards over or under drawers, sometimes combined with fold-out desks; all these were set into the walls of rooms or along corridors and designed to hold bedding, clothing,

ABOVE: Production rocker, c. 1870–1910; ash and maple with black paint and hickory splint seat, New Lebanon, New York. Made for sale to worldly customers, these rockers were produced in many sizes over a long period of time.

RIGHT: Interior of a school room in the Center Family house at Shaker Village, Pleasant Hill, Kentucky. Shaker grammar schools were often open to non-Shaker children.

linens, and other items. The stone dwelling house built at the Enfield, Connecticut, Community in 1841 had no less than 860 individual drawers, nine each for its ninety-five inhabitants.

The architecture of work spaces was equally well thought out. The great stone barn at Hancock, Massachusetts, was round rather than square or rectangular in shape so that cattle in stalls facing the center of the structure might be fed from a single central food source. An early production-line system was established at the Mount Lebanon, New York, Community, which produced chairs for sale to the World, with individual workers specializing in turning, assembling, seating, or staining, at a great savings in time and effort.

In all that the Shakers made, they were influenced by their religious doctrines, striving to create on earth a perfect society which would prove to be both a testimony to their faith and a structure through which it might be realized.

Chapter One

FURNISHING UTOPIA: SHAKER COMMUNITY FURNITURE

Though serious critiques on Shaker furniture appeared as early as 1923, in the prestigious magazine *Antiques,* and the subject was frequently profiled in major magazines and newspapers throughout the 1960s and 1970s, it was not until the 1980s that the general public became aware of this material as having monetary value. At that time a series of auctions of Shaker furnishings produced prices which drew national press coverage. Popular figures in the entertainment world such as Bill Cosby and Oprah Winfrey (who paid $220,000 in 1990 for a work counter) built major collections, while even the most common community pieces brought prices unheard of until that time.

Though the market has cooled off a bit during this decade, Shaker is still a magic word among collectors, a fact which would be viewed with irony if not chagrin by the Believers who, after all, sought only to create simple, useful furnishings. Of course, it is that very simplicity and usefulness which attracts the modern eye.

BEGINNINGS OF THE CRAFT

At the time that the first Shaker communities were established, in the late eighteenth century, the Believers were not well-to-do. They could not afford to purchase furniture. Moreover, the teachings of Mother Ann warned against furnishings that bore "superfluous" decoration, a criticism which would have applied then as now to most furniture. However, there were cabinetmakers and chair turners as well as carpenters among the new converts, and wood was readily available on their newly settled properties. What was made and how it would look was determined not only by religious strictures and community needs but also by the backgrounds of the craftsmen.

Moreover, at the time the first communities were coming together, the prevailing furniture style in both England and the United States was the Classical, here called the

BELOW: Trestle table, c. 1820–1860; maple and oak with wrought-iron braces, New York or New England. Tables such as this, six to twenty feet in length, were used in the communal dining rooms.

LEFT: Building interior Shakertown, Pleasant Hill, Kentucky. Note the unusual cantilevered stairways accenting the open, clean architectural lines.

ABOVE: Dwelling house Shakertown, Pleasant Hill, Kentucky. The cupboards along the wall were used for storage. Floors were kept clear except for an occasional scatter rug.

RIGHT: Child's desk, c. 1815– 1845; pine and cherry, New York or New England. A variation on the traditional schoolmaster's or clerk's desk, but with a Shaker flourish— the rare side-opening drawer.

Federal. Unlike prior modes such the Queen Anne and Chippendale, Federal emphasized relatively plain lines, geometric shapes, and minimal carving. Converts familiar with this look simply eliminated inlay, minimized moldings, and replaced brass knobs and pulls with wooden ones. Thus was born, for the most part, the desired "Shaker look." That this basically eighteenth-century style continued to be popular in the Eastern communities until after the Civil War reflects a combination of religious doctrine and craft tradition.

Elders in the society appear to have had the power to prescribe on furniture design, and the 1845 edition of the Millennial Laws specifically mandated that "furniture of dwelling rooms, among Believers, should be plain in style, and unembellished by stamps, flowers, paintings, and gildings of any kind." Also, after the first years most cabinetmakers were trained within the community (where contact with the outside world was often infrequent) and tended to follow the taste and techniques of their masters.

UNIFORMITY AND INNOVATION

Another important factor tended to favor singular and uniform design. Unlike worldly craftsmen who had to satisfy a clientele often aware of and eager for the latest fashions, Shaker cabinetmakers needed only to satisfy the religious and practical needs of their communities. As these differed greatly from those of the World, very different furniture often resulted.

Since communal eating arrangements were customary, large trestle tables, often 12 to 20 feet long, were produced as well as special low-backed dining chairs. Women working together utilized sewing desks with drawers on all sides rather than the traditional square sewing stand with drawers on only one side, which was in general favor. Washstands might be made to accommodate several people rather than a single person. Beds were mounted on wheels to facilitate cleaning, and the frail and elderly were accommodated in adult-size rocking cradles that had no worldly counterpart.

These and many other innovations in furniture design set Shaker furniture apart. Drawer arrangements in desks, workstands, work counters, cupboards, and shop benches were often unique, specially built to satisfy a particular need. Unlike the prevailing custom, Shaker-made drawers were often placed asymmetrically through balancing equivalent but nonmatching forms rather than following the traditional placement of matching units on each side of an imaginary central axis. What must have seemed bizarre at the time appears to the modern eye to be fairly natural.

Drawers showed up everywhere, often in the most unexpected places—hung beneath the top of a trestle table, between the bracket feet of a traditional six-board chest or chest of drawers, stacked in tiers atop a sewing desk or work counter; in short, wherever they were useful. Much the same may be said for drop leaves, which were added freely to sewing desks, counters, and even cupboards.

Turned wooden pegs for hanging clothing or towels were attached to washstands, tables, and counters. At the time, none of this was customary outside the Shaker community.

Traditional forms like tables and chairs were redesigned to suit particular needs. The common Federal-style tripod-base candlestand was given underhung storage drawers or a narrow molding to produce a spill-proof tray top. Threaded shafts allowed some stands to be raised or lowered. Patented tilters were added to side chairs to avoid floor damage, and shawl bars were

FAR LEFT: Cantilevered stairway in a building at Shakertown, Pleasant Hill, Kentucky. Shaker buildings were designed to provide abundant light and air.

LEFT: Washstand, c. 1820–1850; pine, birch, and maple, traces of old red stain, New York or New England. Washstands were common in American homes prior to the installation of modern plumbing.

FOLLOWING PAGE: Interior of a dwelling house Shakertown, Pleasant Hill, Kentucky, as it would have appeared in the nineteenth century. Note the chairs hung on walls for neatness.

attached to rockers to provide comfort and warmth. A major Shaker innovation was the revolving stool, forerunner of much modern office and shop furniture.

Despite such variations in design, most northeastern Shaker furniture from the pre-1850 period (regarded by many as the sect's "golden age") has a uniformity of appearance that is readily apparent to the knowledgeable. This is due to not only the simple lines and high quality of workmanship but also to the finish.

Finishes such as shellac and paint were touchy subjects with Shaker theologians. The Millennial Laws of 1845 allowed the application of varnish to "moveables,"—tables, chairs, chests, bureaus, and the like—and dictated that particular pieces of furniture, such as bedsteads, could be painted only in certain colors. However, as the nineteenth century progressed, use of finishes on furniture became general practice. Initially pieces were given an opaque coating, generally of red, green, blue, or chrome yellow, sometimes with shellac applied over this to create a shiny surface. Later, transparent oil colors, through which the natural wood grain might be seen, became popular; and at all times a clear shellac or varnish finish was deemed acceptable by most.

But not by all. In 1861 Brother Isaac Newton Youngs of the Mount Lebanon Community complained, "There is a great proclivity in this, our day, for fixing up matters very nice, & the varnish has to go on to the cupboards, drawers, &c & the paint onto floors, everything has to be so slick

ABOVE: The Ministry dining room at Hancock Shaker Village, Massachusetts, showing a trestle table, chairs, and cupboards. The ironstone china on the shelves was not Shaker-made, but, rather, bought from the World.

LEFT: Secretary desk with hinged writing surface, c. 1810–1850; pine, New York or New England. Like much Shaker furniture, this piece was originally built into a wall.

ABOVE: "Retiring" or sleeping room,
Sabbathday Lake Community, Maine.
Note the variety of seating furniture
and footstools. Though frugal, the Shakers
were not opposed to worldly comforts.

RIGHT: Chest of drawers, c. 1810–1850;
pine or poplar, New York or New England.
Though patterned on "worldly" Federal
examples, community chests of drawers are
less elaborate in both form and decoration.

that a fly will slip on it!" Youngs's ideas would fall on deaf ears today, as Shaker furnishings in original paint or colored stain tend to bring the highest prices at auction.

SHAKER ADAPTATIONS

However, not all Shaker-made furniture falls into this category of smoothly rectilinear forms finished in red, yellow, or blue. Settlements located farther west, established later in the century and farther removed from New England influence, often reflected prevailing local taste, which by the 1840s was Empire verging on Victorian.

Groveland, in western New York State, the last Shaker community to be established (in 1826), produced walnut beds, cupboards over drawers, bookcases, desks, and tables with distinctly Victorian characteristics, including paneled sides, Gothic doors, and shaped skirts as well as cupboards with overhung drawers in the Empire manner.

LEFT: Child's commode or wash stand, c. 1820–1860; pine and maple, New England or Midwestern. The Shakers produced miniature furniture for use in the children's orders.

RIGHT: Building interior at Hancock Shaker Village, Massachusetts, showing a large desk of the form often referred to as a "trustees" desk. Note the peg rails running about the walls. Chairs, clothing, and other items could be hung on these.

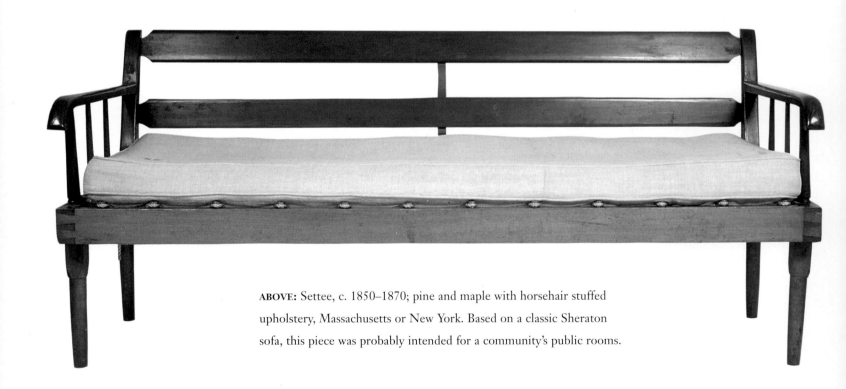

ABOVE: Settee, c. 1850–1870; pine and maple with horsehair stuffed upholstery, Massachusetts or New York. Based on a classic Sheraton sofa, this piece was probably intended for a community's public rooms.

RIGHT: Small cabinet, cupboard over five drawers, c. 1850–1880; pine and butternut, New York, Kentucky or Ohio. Most Shaker cupboards, being made for specific purposes, were unique in design.

Though Union Village, the first of the Ohio communities, was founded in 1805, its craftsmen—like those of the other, smaller Ohio and Indiana settlements—did not always follow eastern dictates in furniture construction. Cupboards and chests of drawers may have bracket feet and scalloped valences in the Federal manner, while the ends of case pieces are paneled and keyhole surrounds are sometimes inlaid in bone. Marble tops were added to the traditional trestle table.

Pleasant Hill (1806) and South Union (1807) in Kentucky produced furnishings which displayed a Southern vernacular influence, including decoratively turned legs, bold projecting moldings, and even figured veneers. The pie safes with decorative punched-tin panels made here are unknown in New England Shaker communities, though they were common throughout the worldly South.

Nor did the eastern settlements remain "pure." After the Civil War more and more Victorian elements appeared in Shaker furniture. In part this mirrored the progressive impact of the surrounding society. It also, however, reflected a desire among the Brethren to remain competitive. As one elder remarked, "the world moves"; and as membership declined in what more and more outsiders regarded as an old-fashioned religious order, Shaker leadership attempted to update the communities. The extent of this change is evident from late-nineteenth- to early-twentieth-century photographs of Shaker interiors, which sometimes appear little different from contemporary Victorian homes.

Ultimately, the effort to update was all in vain; much of the furniture made after 1860 has been rejected by collectors, both because it does not fit their preconception of just what is "Shaker" and because, unless signed

ABOVE: Two-piece "plantation desk" from South Union, Kentucky, consisting of a table upon which is mounted a bookcase or cupboard.

RIGHT: Interior of the Center Family dwelling house, Shakertown, Pleasant Hill, Kentucky, showing a production rocker, candlestand and, at the right, a typical Kentucky Shaker ladder-back rocking chair.

LEFT: Single-drawer stand, c. 1820–1840; butternut, pine, and maple, New York or New Hampshire. The canted legs and drawer front make this an unusual piece.

ABOVE: Center Family dwelling house, Shakertown, Pleasant Hill, Kentucky. Buildings of this design owe much to the Federal architectural style then in vogue in the World.

or determined to be of a firm historical underpinning, the work is often very difficult to identify as community-made. Yet, identifiable pieces are a part of a respected tradition, and more and more are finding their way into museum collections.

THE SHAKER CHAIR INDUSTRY

Though the bulk of their furnishings were made for use within their communities, the Shakers were quick to recognize the opportunity for trade with the World. Harvard, Massachusetts, was selling chairs by 1828, and an 1843 journal entry indicated that nearly one hundred chairs, of assorted types, were then being offered in the village shop. The Alfred, Maine, Community sold tables, stands, and chairs, c. 1802–1817, while the Believers at Union Village, Ohio, were recording chair sales as early as 1813. The Pleasant Hill, Kentucky, settlement sold a table in 1810 and a bureau a year later, and continued to offer tripod-base candlestands for several decades.

There is no evidence, though, that any of these communities produced furniture for general sale in any quantity. The only Shaker society to create an important furniture business was Mount Lebanon, New York, and its craftsmen specialized only in side and armchairs, rockers, and footstools.

Mount Lebanon, in upstate New York near the Massachusetts border, was the largest eastern settlement, the first to be organized (1787), and the location of the sect's central ministry. In its heyday, during the 1860s, it boasted nearly six hundred inhabitants living and working in 125 buildings on six thousand acres of rolling farm and pasture land.

A chair-making industry was established here at an early date. Records indicate that seating furniture was being sold both to worldly buyers and to other communities as far back as 1789, and during the first half of the nineteenth century three Families—the East, Canaan, and Second—had their own shops.

What they produced were side, arm, and rocking chairs of the traditional ladder-back variety, first with rush or splint seats, later with seats of a specially woven textile tape. These pieces were distinguished from ordinary, non-Shaker ladder-backs by refined lines featuring delicately turned posts, pointed oval finials, and lighter rocker blades.

ELDER WAGAN & CO.

Around 1850, the Second Family of Mount Lebanon came to dominate the worldly business, issuing broadsides promoting its products and turning out some two hundred chairs per year, a figure that was increased to six hundred by 1860. This, however, was but a sign of things to come.

In 1863 the South Family (formed to accommodate the overflow from the Second Family) took over the trade under the dynamic leadership of Elder Robert Wagan (1833–1883).

Little is known of Wagan's life, but the following lines from his eulogy printed in the "Shaker Manifesto" for January, 1884, indicate the high regard in which his Brethren held him: "In business with the children of this world, he was prompt and decided, and honest to the last farthing, yet friendly and affable . . . In temporal things we leaned on him as on a staff that could never fail us. As a leader we were sure he would never lead us astray . . . ."

Robert Wagan was a skilled entrepreneur who spotted a market niche that the Shaker craftsmen could fill. Most Victorian furniture was heavy and ornate, hard to move about, and particularly ill-suited for the country and seaside "cottages" then becoming popular among the well-to-do. It was also the day of the verandah, an elongated porch which required many chairs, particularly rockers. Capitalizing on the well-established Shaker reputation for quality and fair price and public familiarity with traditional ladder-back chairs, Wagan established an industry that between 1873 and 1942 turned out tens of thousands of pieces.

At a new factory built by the South Family in 1872, Wagan perfected a simple form of mass production (utilizing steam-powered jigs, duplicating lathes, and boring machinery) which greatly increased output of a standardized but high-grade product. Initially, two thirds of the chairs were rockers, the rest ordinary side and armchairs; only two sizes were available in a single color—mahogany, produced through use of a red logwood dye.

By 1874, however, when Wagan's first catalog was issued, the output was almost solely rockers, which could be purchased in numbered sizes (the numbers were branded into a slat), from a child's "0" to the largest adult rocker, "7." Finished in a red mahogany, ebony, or natural (termed "white") and varnished, the rockers varied in design. The majority were traditional ladder-backs with three or, in larger models, four shaped slats, with woven woolen tape (called worsted lace) seats. These were available with or without arms or an added shawl- or cushion-bar at the crest. Variations included the so-called web-back rockers, which substituted a woven tape for the ladder-back, and upholstered chairs with plush padded backs and seats. The latter are rarely seen today, due to the (invariably) deteriorated fabric having been replaced with tape.

Wagan also manufactured two types of foot-stools, or "foot benches." The more common

BELOW: Revolving stool, c. 1850–1880; maple with pine seat, New Hampshire or Massachusetts. Called "revolvers," these adjustable seats were invented by the Shakers for use in their shops and quickly copied by the World.

RIGHT: Ladder-back side chair, c. 1830–1840; ash and maple, with so-called "egg in cup" finials, Kentucky.

LEFT: "Retiring" or sleeping room, with a typical Shaker cast-iron stove, two single beds, and a side chair hung, as usual, from the pegboard.

LEFT: In this set of rooms at Hancock Shaker Village, the woodwork has been painted in a lovely shade of blue—providing a pleasing contrast to the whitewashed walls.

ABOVE: Kitchen at Hancock Shaker Village, Massachusetts, showing a work table, an unusual sink, and built-in cupboards. Note the interior window shutters.

example had an oblong, slightly canted body and four turned legs joined on the long side by stretchers. The other type, referred to as a "two-step bench," looked like a short set of stairs. Both could be purchased either plain or covered with cushioned fabric.

SHAKER COMPETITION

Mount Lebanon Shaker products proved so popular that they were soon copied by non-Shaker manufacturers. Wagan, in his 1874 catalog, found it necessary to caution the buying public that "there are now several manufacturers of chairs who have made and introduced into market an imitation of our styles of chairs, which they sell for Shakers' Chairs and which are unquestionably bought by the public generally under the impression that they are the real genuine article."

In an attempt to circumvent such copying the Shakers marked their chairs with an oval decal in the form of a gold transfer, reading:

Shakers' Trade Mark
Mt. Lebanon, N.Y.

and featuring an illustration of a Shaker armless rocker. Most such decals, however, have now disappeared from the chairs.

By 1876, output had increased to three thousand units per year, and it continued strong into this century with chairs being sold through such major department stores as Philadelphia's John Wanamaker's and Marshall Field of Chicago. However, the five-story factory building burned in 1923. The business was reestablished in smaller quarters, by Brother William Perkins (d. 1934), but a dwindling work force and unavailability of tape due to the wartime emergency brought it to an end in 1942.

Thousands of these Shaker-produced side chairs and rockers have survived, though, and these readily recognizable pieces are what most collectors associate with the term Shaker furniture. Examples in common sizes, refinished or with replaced tape, often may be purchased for a few hundred dollars, thus making them the least expensive today of all Shaker furniture forms.

ABOVE: The massive stove and ovens in the kitchen at Hancock Shaker Village, Massachusetts, were designed for institutional cooking.

FOLLOWING PAGE:
Dining chairs, c. 1840–1860; maple and ash or hickory, New York or New England. These unusual low-back chairs had only a single slat. They were used at the trestle tables in community dining rooms.

Chapter Two

USEFUL AND NECESSARY:
SHAKER WOODENWARE

It may be difficult for those of us living in a world of department stores and shopping malls to comprehend the desire that the Shakers (and their worldly neighbors) expressed for hand-made objects. Yet most of what they used in their living quarters, kitchens, shops, and fields was manufactured in the communities by trained craftsmen; and much of it was made of wood, currently a material largely displaced by plastics, glass, ceramics, and metals.

Many of these useful objects were intended only for home use, but some, such as the famous Shaker oval boxes and carriers, were also offered for sale to outsiders. Today, both items are eagerly sought by collectors despite the fact that many Shaker-made wooden utensils are very difficult to distinguish from similar examples produced outside the faith.

SHAKER TRADE

In order to appreciate the Shaker woodenware industry it is important to know something of the Believers' attitude toward trade in general. Each Shaker Family was initially free to produce whatever it felt was necessary for survival. However, inevitably, differences in inclination, skills, and available materials led to certain Families dominating certain crafts. For example, the Second and, later, the South Family of Mount Lebanon were the chief chairmakers, while seed boxes were a specialty at Union Village, Ohio. Items left over after community needs had been satisfied might be sold to the World, but only under certain conditions. First, they must be of a quality equal to those used by the Shakers themselves. They would sell no inferior goods. Second, business could be transacted only by certain community members.

The Shakers feared moral contamination from the worldly, so only the most sound individuals, known as Trustees and appointed by the Elders, were allowed to trade with outside interests. This was clearly spelled out by the 1845 revisions to the Millennial Laws: "It is the duty of the Deacons and Deaconesses, or Trustees, to see to the domestic concerns of the Family in which they reside, and to perform all business transaction, either with the World, or with believers in other families or societies."

BELOW: Broom straw stored in a community workshop. The Shakers developed the modern straw broom, and for years they grew broom straw and manufactured fine brooms for use and sale.

LEFT: Storage area, showing a detail of a built-in high chest. Like this one, many Shaker chests and cupboards were set into the walls to conserve space and promote neatness.

Each Family had its own store, under Trustee supervision, where a wide variety of products were offered to non-Believers. Business was conducted always on a cash basis, as the Shakers did not believe in credit, though barter was permissible and practiced often.

Not all, however, was sold through the stores. A much wider market was reached through a consignment of goods sold on commission by worldly agencies, wholesale distribution to agents in larger cities, and the establishing of trade routes to both solicit orders and deliver goods. These goods were turned out in numerous shops staffed by Brothers who initially had learned their skills before conversion but more often, as the years passed, who had been trained within the communities. Shakers customarily learned several skills rather than a single one, as it was believed that "variety of occupation is a source of plea-

ABOVE: Covered carrier, c. 1870–1920; pine and maple, Mount Lebanon, New York. Such carriers are actually oval storage boxes with applied handles. They were popular tourist items.

sure." This diversity of skills stood the sect in good stead in later years as membership dwindled and Brethren had to assume new tasks.

OVAL BOXES

Oval wooden storage boxes have long been one of the most readily identifiable and desirable of Shaker collectibles. However, long-time enthusiasts were still astonished when small (6 to 8 inch) boxes in paint brought $10,000 and more at auction in the 1980s and early 1990s. While these prices may be largely attributed to clever promotion and naive, nouveau-riche customers, the fact remains that the oval box stands as a leitmotif of the Shaker culture.

While Believers were not the only ones to make such boxes they were among the first (in around 1800) to do so, and their examples are unquestionably the finest. Sold in nesting sets of 5, 7, 9, or 12, they were produced in great quantity at Mount Lebanon, New York, until the 1930s and, thereafter, by Brother Delmar Wilson of Sabbathday Lake, Maine, until 1961.

RIGHT: View of a room at Hancock Shaker Village, Massachusetts, showing the intricate built-in cupboards and drawers so characteristic of community interiors.

The oval tops and bottoms were cut from thin pine boards, and the birch or maple sides, or "rims," were steamed or soaked until they were flexible enough to be bent in an oval and secured to top and bottom with wooden pegs. Unlike most worldly boxes, which were nailed flush at the lap, Shaker boxes were cut into long fingers (lappers), which were then secured with copper rivets. By 1834, sizes were standardized, and the 1845 revision to the Millennial Laws directed that "oval or nice boxes may be stained reddish or yellow." Examples in green and blue are also found as well as the more common varnish finish. It should also be kept in mind that many oval boxes were painted and decorated by purchasers, so one cannot always be sure that the paint work is in fact "Shaker paint."

The same form, with a loop handle and with or without a cover, was termed a carrier, and many of these were made into sewing baskets, padded and lined in colored silk damask and fitted out with matching fittings, emeries, pincushions, beeswax, and needle cases. From the number that have survived, it would appear that such oval sewing boxes and carriers were among the most popular of twentieth-century store products. Much rarer were round-fingered carriers, an unpainted example of which sold at auction in 1988 for $8,000. Collectors should also bear in mind that both oval boxes and carriers are being reproduced today, and that modern products have, in some cases, been passed off as older, authentic examples.

OTHER SHAKER BOXES

The Shakers had need for many other box forms, some of which were also sold to the World. Rectangular open wooden boxes with loop handles and square machine-dovetailed corners were termed "oblong carriers" in catalogs. They are seldom seen today. There were also round bent-wood boxes lapped in the worldly manner. Some, with covers, were used for dry storage or for keeping cheese. They should not be confused with the measures in graduated sizes that lacked a cover and that often bore a stenciled Shaker logo and a capacity mark.

Measures, important both on the farm and in grist mills, were being sold by 1790. In 1806, a set of three measures (termed a "seat of meashers") cost ten shillings. They were a specialty of the Hancock, Massachusetts, Community, as were the large round spittoons which, filled with wood shavings, caught the tobacco chewer's effluvia. These latter brought a quarter each in 1839. Other specialized containers included sugar boxes made in nesting sizes and boxes for spool storage.

Most utilitarian boxes were left unpainted, varnished, or merely given a coat of red; however, a few covered examples, offered for worldly sale, were given polychrome paper surfaces. The Shakers also produced large quantities of cardboard and heavy paper boxes to use in shipping herbs, garden seeds, and various homeopathic medicines.

BELOW: Two round spice boxes, c. 1840–1880; pine and birch in old blue paint, New England. Though best known for their oval boxes, the Shakers also made many round ones.

LEFT: A stack of nineteenth- and twentieth-century birch and pine bent-wood storage boxes with laped construction typical of the Mount Lebanon, New York, Community.

BUCKETS, PAILS, AND BARRELS

A wide variety of buckets, pails, barrels, churns, and firkins, referred to as "coopers" ware, were produced in Shaker shops. Here, too, there was community specialization. Enfield, New Hampshire, was famous for the pine sap buckets made at a shop set up in 1866 by Elder Henry Cumings of the North Family and maintained until 1892.

Made of staves bound together with iron hoops and bearing a sheet-iron hanging tab within the rim, these buckets were customarily painted red inside and out, and were often impressed on the bottom:

N.F. Shakers
Enfield, N.H.

ABOVE: Two types of wooden bucket and a broom, all typical of the useful objects produced by the Shakers for the communities as well as for sale to the World.

RIGHT: Churn, c. 1800–1820; maple and hickory with wrought nails, New York, probably Watervliet. The fine lapping is an early version of the technique later employed on oval boxes.

ABOVE: Carrier, c. 1850–1880; ash and maple painted red, New England. These box-like carriers were used to hold herbs gathered for medicinal purposes and flowers collected for their seeds.

Collectors consider the marked examples especially desirable. Cumings's shop also turned out covered pails with wire-bail handles set in diamond-shaped iron sockets, which are regarded as a sign of Shaker manufacture even in unmarked examples. Pails made at other settlements came in three standard sizes and were often used for selling Shaker foodstuffs such as apple butter.

Wooden churns for making butter (an important product of the Alfred, Maine, colony until 1850) and large, iron-bound staved tubs with cut-out handles were made in many Shaker shops. The latter served many purposes, as evidenced by Mount Lebanon records which, between 1789 and 1831, list sales of the following: "die" (dye) tubs, meat tubs, wash tubs, sugar tubs, beer tubs, and cheese tubs. Small tubs, called firkins, were used to store butter and lard. Barrels and boxes were also produced in quantity, but surviving examples can seldom be identified as Shaker.

RIGHT: Covered bucket or firkin, c. 1890-1920; pine in blue paint, Maine or Massachusetts. The use of metal staples to secure the laps rather than nails or pegs indicates that this is a later product.

LEFT: Shaker-attributed covered bucket, c. 1880–1910; pine painted yellow with sheet-iron banding, New England. It is often difficult to distinguish Shaker-made items from those produced in surrounding communities.

OTHER WOODENWARE

The Shakers produced many other useful wooden objects including some, such as dippers and funnels, which we are accustomed to seeing today made from different materials. Dippers were sold at Mount Lebanon as early as 1789 and continued to be produced there throughout much of the nineteenth century. Made of ash and maple, they looked like a round measure with a turned handle set into the side at an angle. Collectors often confuse the Shaker product with a very similar-looking dipper still produced at Frye's Measure Mill near Wilton, New Hampshire. Fortunately, the Frye examples are customarily branded on the base:

Old Time
Woodenware
Frye's Measure Mill
Wilton, N.H.

LEFT: Hand-carved hardwood hay fork and grain shovel from the mid- to late nineteenth century; both from South Union, Kentucky. Even such utilitarian objects as these show typical Shaker care and artistry.

ABOVE: Room in a building at Shaker Village-West, Stockbridge, Massachusetts, with examples of community-made wooden kitchenware and baskets.

RIGHT: Covered or traveling mirror, c. 1870–1900; pine and glass, New York or New England. Typical of Shaker practicality, the hinged cover protects the mirror. These pieces are today less common than Shaker hand mirrors.

BELOW: Hand mirrors, c. 1880–1920; pine with traces of old stain, and glass, New York or New England. Though some claim that these graceful looking-glasses were purchased from the World, they show a characteristic Shaker form.

LEFT: Exterior of a nineteenth-century building at Canterbury Shaker Village, New Hampshire. Gambrel roof buildings like this are uncommon in Shaker architecture.

Frye also produced another object often taken for Shaker, though never produced by the Believers. This is an oblong knife box with bent-wood sides and a central carrying handle. Shaker knife boxes were rectangular with a central divider pierced by three finger holes or a slot. Another interesting look-alike is the well-known Shaker apple-butter scoop, an elongated shovel-like utensil with a d-shaped handle carved from the same block of wood. There is no doubt that Believers produced these, but remarkably similar examples have been made for centuries in southern Italy.

Among the most distinctive of Shaker woodenware are clothes hangers. These bear little resemblance to modern-day ones, which in most cases are spatula-like or slightly curved pieces of flattened wood with a central hole for a hanging cord. An interesting variation is the multiple hanger with two or three such bars set at right angles to a vertical hanging shaft. Shaker craftsmen are also said to have developed a type of wooden clothespin, and in 1876 their newly invented wooden washing machine won a bronze medal at the Philadelphia Centennial Exposition, hailed for its "size, strength, simplicity, and capability for extensive uses."

Many Shaker household implements were lathe-turned on the water-powered machinery found in most communities. Among these are funnels, rolling pins, mortars and pestles, mashers of various sorts, spoons, spatulas, scoops, mallets, and a great variety of spools, some for common thread and others, much larger, for use in weaving. Those who appreciate Shaker craftsmanship always marvel at the fact that even such mundane objects as spools are so beautifully shaped. Another such object is the Shaker carpet beater, made in some quantity around 1900 at Mount Lebanon. A lesson in simplicity, it consisted of a bent-wood loop set into a turned handle. Nothing could be simpler, but it did the job as well as any factory-made Victorian iron-wire beater.

One of the sect's "best-sellers" in the Trustees' stores was the turned walnut or maple sewing stand, a small shaped pedestal topped with a felt pincushion and set upon a round base, from

FOLLOWING PAGE:
Broom-making shop at Shakertown, Pleasant Hill, Kentucky. The reenactor is binding a broom in the old manner. Note the stacks of handles and bundles of broom straw.

which protruded iron rods to hold spools of thread. There were also turned maple darning eggs and swifts, adjustable devices for measuring yarn which could be clamped to a work surface. For decades these latter items were a popular product of the Hancock shops, sold widely both here and in the British Isles.

Also much in demand were the two basic Shaker mirrors: a hand mirror with oval glass and tapering handle and an ingenious traveling mirror, with the looking-glass surface completely protected by a hinged wooden cover. Both types were turned out in cherrywood and in black-painted or "ebonized" pine. The hand mirrors are found in graduated sizes from tiny, doll-like miniatures at four inches long to those up to a foot in length; the traveling mirrors appear to have been made only in a single dimension.

Students in the sect's schools were fitted out not only with steel pens invented by the faithful but also with slates, miniature blackboards made of a piece of thin red or black slate set in a narrow pine

ABOVE: Scoop, c. 1840–1870; carved maple, New York or New England. This is one of the most graceful and innovative Shaker forms, and one most sought after by collectors.

LEFT: Grain or apple shovel, c. 1830–1870; carved maple, New York or New England. Like other farmers, the Shakers used wooden shovels to avoid striking sparks in the barn and to avoid bruising apples.

or cherry frame pegged together at the corners. Many of these still bear the initials of the scholar, as this sort of identification was deemed proper under the Millennial Laws.

Large wool or "walking" wheels and smaller flax wheels for spinning were made at Canterbury, New Hampshire, from 1815 onwards as well as clock reels used to measure yarn. Seldom marked, without a reliable history it is often difficult to distinguish these from worldly products. Additionally, massive cheese presses were made as were the broom vises devised to assist in the broom-making industry, which following invention of the flat broom by Brother Theodore Bates of Watervliet became a major source of income. Broom corn was first grown here in 1798, and by 1805 brooms were also being made at Mount Lebanon where they sold for thirty to fifty cents apiece.

The Shakers made many types of brooms as well as selling turned broom and mop handles. They also produced a variety of brushes and feather dusters with delicately shaped handles. The Trustee Daniel J. Hawkins was in charge of the Mount Lebanon business, and his initials—*D. H.*—will be found set into the bristles of some of the brushes made there. Types listed in sales inventories of the period include lather or shaving, shoe, scrubbing, paint, and "dust" [pan] brushes. Except, perhaps, for quality of workmanship, most of these were little different from brushes made in the shops of non-Believers.

Among the Shaker woodenware items least likely to be recognized as Shaker-made are those developed for use in the various trades carried on by the Believers. For example, there are shallow square boxes with open slat bottoms and two loop handles, which were designed to carry bottles for patent medicines, as well as the triangular, nail-studded frames on which the bottles were dried. There are also the numerous sawn and carved wooden glove, mitten, and sock forms used by the Sisters who made such items both for community use and

ABOVE: Pedestal-form covered storage container, c. 1880–1920; turned from mixed woods, New York or New England. Yet another of the attractive small novelty items offered to visitors at the trustees' stores on community grounds.

sale, in addition to the attractive hat and bonnet forms (each Brother and Sister had an individual one) utilized in making headgear. A really hard item to spot is the tiny "shampoo comb," a section of imported bamboo with tiny teeth cut in one end. Sold in Shaker shops, these were probably intended to aid in removing head lice.

Many other wooden devices were made for use on the farm and in the buttery. Since few of these were sold to outsiders (at least while the communities remained active), they are both hard to find and harder still to recognize. Small butter presses with iron clamps were used to make one-pound blocks. However, the colorful molds featuring flowers, birds, and animals so popular among others were apparently not used by the Shakers, as they were believed too decorative.

ABOVE: Mortar and pestle, c. 1840–1870; turned and painted pine, Ohio. The Shakers raised medicinal herbs and made a number of home remedies. Herbs were often ground in a mortar such as this.

LEFT: Heart-shaped maple sugar mold, c. 1840–1870; carved pine with iron nails, Massachusetts. The Northeastern communities had large maple groves and produced syrup both for sale and home consumption.

Turned wooden apple corers and peelers, simple in concept but lovely in design, were employed in the important cider and dried-apple business, as was a benchlike form set with an iron blade with which to slice corn kernels from the cob, and hand presses for extracting juice from the many fruits grown in every community. Small pine berry boxes with ventilation holes in the sides were used to gather and ship much of this fruit.

These listed items, while varied and many, are hardly exhaustive of the vast quantity of wooden objects produced in the various Shaker communities. Since most of these were never marked, for identification, the collector must rely on history, comparison with similar examples in museum collections, and a general "feel" for the material, which comes only from long exposure to Shaker craftsmanship.

ABOVE: Woodworking planes, c. 1850–1900; pine and maple with steel blades. The Shakers were skilled craftsmen, not only building their own communities but also making the tools with which they worked.

RIGHT: Cabinet containing a variety of carpenter's tools and molding planes used by sect craftsmen.

Chapter Three

METALWORK, BASKETS, AND SIEVES: SHAKER CRAFTS

I f their goal of economic independence was to be realized, the Shakers understood that they must be more than an agricultural community, that they also must be able to produce the fabricated metal objects—as well as household specialty items such as baskets—which other farmers and the general public routinely purchased from foundries, smiths, and tinkers.

IRONWORK

Smiths and other mechanics had been among the order's earliest adherents, and within the community they quickly expanded their traditional role, creating in some cases small factories with the most advanced power-driven equipment. The cut nail (a machined product which soon replaced the hand-wrought nails of antiquity) is said to have been invented by Sister Sarah Babbit of the Harvard Community, and was being sold to the World by 1788. Records of the Mount Lebanon Community for the following year indicate production of such diverse items as hinges, latches, gates, scythes, knifes, hoes, and a great variety of iron tools both for home use and sale to the general public.

At Mount Lebanon, water power motivated a great trip-hammer to pound metal into shape and drove the numerous lathes employed in turning out the metal parts for such needed equipment as looms, silk-reeling machines, water wheels, and threshing machines.

Any visitor to Shaker restorations such as Hancock, Massachusetts, or Pleasant Hill, Kentucky, can observe the effect of this industry. The hinges on the doors, the fences, the iron foot scrapers at the stoops, the window latches, all are Shaker-made. Yet the collector seeking authentic community iron work is usually stymied in the matter of identification.

LEFT: Interior at Hancock Shaker Village, Massachusetts, showing a variety of furnishings including work tables, chairs, and a corner cupboard. Shaker tinware and baskets hang from peg rails on the walls.

RIGHT: Interior of the brick dwelling house at Hancock Shaker Village, Massachusetts, showing build-in cupboards and a Shaker iron stove. Community stoves were highly advanced for their time.

BELOW: Several cast-iron "sad irons" used at South Union, Kentucky, during the nineteenth century. Though used by the Shakers, these were probably crafted at a worldly foundry.

Once removed from its societal context most Shaker iron looks very much like much of what was being produced at the time in surrounding villages.

A more readily identifiable group of Shaker cast-iron objects are gravestones. In the mid-nineteenth century such cast examples replaced those of shaped granite or sandstone. Needless to say, these memorials are not collectible, and any seen on the market may be presumed to have been stolen from a graveyard.

SHAKER STOVES

The sect regarded fireplaces as antiquated, dirty, and above all dangerous. Cast-iron box stoves for heating were one of the first products from their foundries. Unlike the ornate examples popular in the World, Shaker stoves were severely functional, lacking any curvilinear decorative elements. Oblong with sides sloping at a slight angle, a wide apron to catch sparks, and a tall sheet-metal smoke pipe, they were set upon long, straight, or slightly curving legs with pad or "penny" feet. Most were made for specific uses in specific places, thus few are actually alike. Yet so faithfully do all adhere to the rule "form follows function" that once the collector sees one, all other examples become recognizable despite the fact that they lack a maker's mark.

Cook stoves, either purchased or shop-made, were fitted with innovations designed to meet the needs of communities required to serve a large number of meals at one time. For example,

LEFT: Nineteenth-century buildings at Canterbury Shaker Village, New Hampshire. Wood frame structures were often painted white. The row of dormers provided light and air for the upper story.

LEFT: Cut-stone farm deacon's shop, built in 1809 and still standing at Shakertown, Pleasant Hill, Kentucky. Note the massive end chimney.

LEFT: "Retiring" or sleeping room, showing a washstand with pitcher and bowl, towel rack, and an unusual mirror suspended from the pegboard. Shaker living areas contained only the basic necessities.

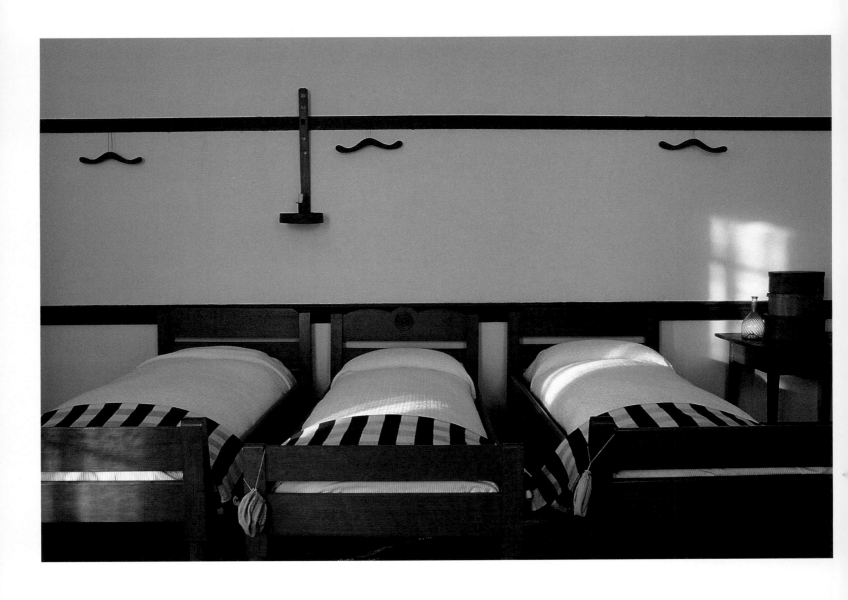

ABOVE: "Retiring" or sleeping room, Shakertown, Pleasant Hill, Kentucky. Distinctive Shaker-made hangers and a candle sconce are suspended from molding on the whitewashed walls.

a stove at Canterbury, New Hampshire, had a built-in soup or stew kettle, while another great kettle at Hancock had a water pipe running directly from the village water tank. Many of these kitchen and laundry stoves were built-in and thus were destroyed with the buildings which housed them. This and their greater size accounts for their present rarity. The smaller heating stoves, on the other hand, come on the market fairly often. One made in Harvard, Massachusetts, brought $4,675 at auction in 1991, while an Enfield, New Hampshire, example sold for $1,100 a year earlier.

TINWARE

Lead-coated sheet iron, or tinware, the forerunner of plastic as a lightweight, durable material, was another important product of the Shaker shops. Canterbury, New Hampshire, was an early center of such products, with workers employing standard patterns to cut from sheet tin the components of a wide variety of vessels. These individual elements were then crimped and soldered together. However, unlike the decorated toleware popular with worldly buyers during the nineteenth century, Shaker tin was left unpainted, or "raw."

A great variety of household and kitchen objects as well as some shop items were produced in this material. Among the pieces known to be Shaker-made are wall-hung match safes, milk pails, kettles, cooking pots, oil cans, and long-spouted kerosene lamp fillers, scoops, dippers, plates, milk pans, pitchers, and coffee pots, funnels, spatulas, and several types of dustpans. One of the latter, a standing type with long handle, sold at auction in 1985 for $500.

Lighting devices were also customarily made of tin. The Millennial Laws set strict rules about the use of candles and lamps, and the preferred lighting device was initially an enclosed lantern with a punched-tin body or glass panels. These were fairly efficient and relatively safe. At a later date, kerosene lamps were set in tin sconces, utilizing tin reflectors.

Shaker tinware was widely sold throughout New England and New York, where its fine quality was welcome to those who had purchased objects offered by the wandering Connecticut tinkers whose legendary trickery has provided the material for so many folktales. Unfortunately, though, these plain but honest Shaker pieces are hard to distinguish from similar worldly wares.

ABOVE: Tin utensils, including maple sugar molds, a colander, lamp filler, bucket, and a sausage stuffer with a pine plunger, all c. 1870–1900; soldered sheet tin, New York or New England. Though made in some quantity, Shaker tin was never marked and it is hard to identify.

FOLLOWING PAGE:
Furnishings assembled in the home of well-known Shaker authorities, Faith and Edward Deming Andrews, who were among the first to study and preserve the Shaker heritage.

LEFT: A brass and walnut pill roller used in the dispensary at South Union, Kentucky. During the nineteenth century the Shakers had an extensive business in herbal and homeopathic medicines.

OTHER METALWORK

Shaker craftsmen are known to have also worked in copper and brass, though few of these products can now be identified. Buttons were being cast or stamped from these metals before 1800, and brass skimmers with wrought-iron handles are known to exist. Then, in 1817, Brother Isaac Youngs of Mount Lebanon invented the first metal writing-pen nibs. These were cut at first from brass and later from silver. Though they sold for a rather pricey twenty-five cents each in 1820, these pens were such an improvement on the traditional quill pens that they found a ready market. Though eventually replaced by mass-produced steel pen nibs, the Shaker product was still in use in the late nineteenth century. In fact, G. A. Loomis of Watervliet used an 1819 nib to write a letter in 1878.

LEFT: Brass and iron wool comb used at South Union, Kentucky, during the 1800s. Wool production was an important industry at several Shaker communities.

SHAKER BASKETRY

Baskets—today perhaps of no great importance—in past decades in most households were indispensable. They were made to some extent in all Shaker communities, while in a few they became important sale items. One source claims that the Church Family of Mount Lebanon produced over seventy thousand baskets during the nineteenth century, a substantial quantity considering that each was handmade and the occupation was only seasonal.

Over the past two decades Shaker-made baskets have become something of a fad among certain collectors, with desirable examples (such as a Sister's four-handled laundry basket which brought $3,200 at auction in 1987) commanding prices in the $2,000–$4,000 range. While such figures do not seem unreasonable in light of the much higher amounts regularly paid for Shaker furniture and oval boxes, it gives one pause to realize that few of these baskets are marked or have a reliable community history. Moreover, as evidenced by records kept at the Hancock settlement, Believers not only made baskets, they regularly bought them from outside manufacturers. Sorting them out can be a problem.

Those who have studied Shaker basketry and profess to be able to distinguish the Believers' products maintain that they can be recognized by the high quality of the splint material used (i.e., smooth and unbroken, of equal width), the fine tooling on the handles and rims, their symmetry, and their uniformity. The latter was achieved through use of molds over which the baskets were woven. Shaker records and existent examples indicate that dozens of different basket types were produced, an understandable situation in a society where agricultural, shop, and domestic use placed high priority on light, durable containers. All of these types can be broken down into two broad categories: utility and "fancy" baskets.

The utility-style baskets were generally larger vessels designed for specific tasks and often made of heavy splint for heavy work. There were handled field baskets, the larger ones for gathering apples and potatoes and smaller ones for berries, herbs, or eggs. The latter often had a high center or "kick up" to distribute the weight and prevent breakage. Also, every Brother and

BELOW: Apple basket, c. 1870–1910; hardwood slats nailed in place, New York or New England. The Shakers grew much fruit and for many years sold both sweet and hard cider.

RIGHT: Two woven nineteenth-century splint baskets from the South Union, Kentucky, Community. Since they were rarely marked, Shaker baskets lacking a community history are hard to identify.

Sister had a two- or four-handled laundry basket, and low oblong baskets were sometimes used for storing clothing.

There were also some highly specialized baskets, the use of which would be unknown to most collectors. Shell-shaped, semicircular splint baskets were used in winnowing grain (it was tossed in the air where the wind would separate the lighter chaff from the grain), tubular baskets served as eel and fish traps, and long flat drying baskets with low rims were filled with sliced apples or pears, then suspended above a stove or placed in a window. Every stove had a leather-lined chip basket for kindling, and shallow baskets with a coarse hexagonal weave were used in the dairy to store wheels of cheese.

These and others were made and used in quantity. They were also sold to the World. The Believers at Alfred, Maine, were offering them as early as 1801, and documents at Mount Lebanon indicate a wide variety of sales between 1809 and 1855. After 1850, though, the business in utility basketry was gradually superseded by a more lucrative market in smaller, more delicate fancy baskets.

Basketmaking is a labor intensive task, involving several steps—the selection, hewing, and soaking (in order for the annular rings to separate) of suitable oak, ash, or hickory trees; the riving or cutting off of long, thin splints suitable for baskets; and the weaving of these splints into the final product.

ABOVE: The weaving shop at Shaker Village-West, Stockbridge, Massachusetts, showing basketmaking tools and equipment as well as reproduction baskets in various stages of preparation.

LEFT: Two nineteenth-century bent-wood grain measures, one iron-bound for greater durability. Both are attributed to the South Union, Kentucky, Community.

ABOVE: Three field or utility baskets of finely woven splint from South Union, c. 1870–1900; Kentucky. Delicacy and strength are combined in these simple carriers.

RIGHT: Double-top fruit basket, c. 1880–1920; hardwood slats nailed together, New York or New England. These unusual baskets were employed both in gathering fruit and displaying it for sale.

The Shakers became extremely proficient manufacturers of such products as baskets due to their customary introduction of labor-saving devices. They employed a trip-hammer, as early as 1816, to crush logs and free the splint. They also introduced metal tanks in which wood could be steamed for flexibility, as well as slitting knifes which enabled the craftsman to cut splints to uniform widths. Special saws and planes were employed to shape handles and rims. And, perhaps most important, wooden molds were utilized efficiently to shape bodies, handles, and rims, thus achieving a uniformity of size and appearance often lacking in the products of non-Believers.

Despite all this, by mid-century their market was slowly being usurped by mass-produced factory-made baskets. Though not as well constructed as community products, these were also of uniform size and they were less expensive. The Shakers looked elsewhere for a market. While continuing to make some utility baskets for community use and local trade, they moved vigorously into the field of fancy basketry, an area previously dominated by Native Americans, chiefly the Iroquois and the Penobscot tribes.

"FANCY" WARE

The term "fancy" basket implies a frivolity quite inappropriate to the Shaker mentality. Believers, in fact, took the term to refer to smaller, lighter baskets designed primarily for use in

LEFT: Fancy or notions basket, c. 1900–1930; woven ash splint in varying sizes, Maine. Adapted from Maine Indian baskets, such delicate pieces were made in great variety for sale to the World.

BELOW: Picnic basket, c. 1890–1920; woven split reed, straw, and hickory splint with a pine bottom, New York or New England. Such baskets were probably modeled on earlier Chinese export rice straw examples.

LEFT: Two fruit-drying baskets, c. 1840–1880; hickory splint, Connecticut. Sliced fruit, usually apples or pears, was placed on these trays and left to dry in the sun or over a stove.

the home and, as they insisted in their advertising materials, "of superior grade, extra fine," and suitable for a "select patronage." Naturally they were more expensive.

A new type of basketry also meant a new group of basketmakers. Traditionally, among the Shakers as in the World, basketmaking had been men's work. Preparation of materials was arduous and even the weaving of a large storage basket of coarse splint could be exhausting labor. Smaller baskets required small hands, dexterity, and skills similar to those employed in knitting or rug hooking. The Sisters became weavers, while the Brothers continued to prepare the splint and make up rims and handles. It was seasonal work, done during the quiet months from November to April, and it must have been pleasurable, for a community scribe notes that at Mount Lebanon even the members of the ministry were known to "labor at basket-making in the intervals of their travels and ministrations."

The new styles also dictated new materials. The finely finished hickory splints now used were only an eighth of an inch wide, and to these delicate wands were joined even more fragile materials—sweet grass (long a popular Native American material), oat straw, Cuban palm leaf, raffia from the far East, and even horsehair.

New forms appeared. Sewing baskets were made in great variety, some of oat straw with covers and swing handles, others (from the Sabbathday Lake Community) in a simple round form but wonderfully light due to their construction of horsehair and sweet grass. Oblong straw or splint picnic baskets with two lids, which opened separately, were very popular. The open hexagonal weave employed in cheese baskets was adapted in hickory for small table or fruit display baskets, and flat basketry trays with a loop handle served to carry in cut flowers. There were even such novelties as tiny, one-inch-high baskets for thimble storage, straw table mats, and raffia fans.

The great majority of this production, which lasted into the early twentieth century, was intended for sale to the World, not only from the Trustees' stores where it was offered to tourists eager to view the "odd" Shaker lifestyle, but also through department stores and specialty shops in locales as far flung as New York City, Chicago, Sacramento, California, and even Nottingham, England.

BELOW: Cheese basket, c. 1830–1860; ash splint in octagonal weave, New Lebanon, New York. Newly-made cheese was placed in these containers in order to drain off the whey. Though seemingly flimsy, such baskets are quite sturdy.

SIEVES

Sieves, lacking the glamour of baskets, were always utilitarian in nature but their production was an important source of income for several Shaker settlements, particularly Mount Lebanon. Finer sieves were used in the household for such things as sifting flour while large, coarsely woven sieves, termed riddles, were employed in sorting and sizing garden and flour seeds. Substantial quantities of specialized examples were also sold to the pharmaceutical and chemical industries.

The earliest sales records date to 1810, and twenty years later the trade at Mount Lebanon was in the hands of the Second and South Families and their superintendent, Daniel J. Hawkins, a

ABOVE: Miniature picnic basket, woven straw and split cane, c. 1890–1930; New England. These novelty items were sold to visitors through the Shaker stores. Some were made in the communities, others were imported from Asia.

man also active in the making of brushes. Under his guidance the business prospered for several decades.

Shaker sieves were made with round, bent-wood frames of ash, across which was stretched a mesh bound in place with textile tape and brass rivets. The finer mesh was woven on looms by the Sisters from silk thread and hair from horses' manes and cows' tails, while a coarser product used in grain and seed riddles was manufactured from iron or copper wire. Both types were made in graduated sizes, and specialized examples were fitted with loop handles or small feet to lift them clear of the work surface. Like baskets, sieves were rarely marked or otherwise identified as Shaker; unlike the former, however, sieves have not been studied in any detail. Consequently, other than examples in museum collections, it is extremely difficult to identify community-made examples.

BELOW: Sewing basket, c. 1880–1910; woven splint, New York or New England. Finely matched hickory splint and careful weaving distinguish the products of Shaker basketmakers.

RIGHT: Two woven straw and splint baskets, one with a leather carrier, c. 1847–1892; Kentucky.

Chapter Four

WOVEN WELL:
SHAKER TEXTILES

Despite the sheer volume of textile objects made by the various Shaker communities, far less is known of this field of workmanship. Moreover, collector interest is such that the sale at auction of a round, hooked rug for $1,200 in 1991 was greeted with some surprise. This moderate interest is due at least in part to the fact that the Shakers both made and purchased fabrics, and the latter are often indistinguishable from the former.

Certain items, however, can be recognized as Shaker-made. Community rugs and bed coverings show a sense of order in design with simple, symmetrical, and repeating patterns. Some items of clothing, such as the well known "Dorothy Cloaks," have unique and recognizable features. The field is an interesting and relatively unexplored one, holding many pleasant surprises for the studious collector.

BED COVERINGS

The institutional arrangement of Shaker sleeping quarters mandated large numbers of sheets, blankets, and coverlets, most of which were woven on community looms. Up until 1830 this was men's work, but thereafter it fell to the Sisters' lot.

As one would expect, Shaker bedding was not elaborately decorated. Bed sheets were of plain linen or cotton, while blankets were usually dyed blue, gray, or in a check pattern, most often blue, black, or red on a white ground. This reflected Millennial Laws requiring that

BELOW: Woven geometric coverlet, c. 1840–1870; indigo-dyed wool and cotton, New York or New England. Shaker coverlets were made on the same looms as worldly examples and are largely indistinguishable from the latter.

RIGHT: A Sister's gown and bonnet, both nineteenth-century. The garment covering the shoulders was called a Bertha.

RIGHT: Shag rug, c. 1880–1910; dyed unraveled machine- or hand-knit wool on mattress ticking backing, Maine or Massachusetts. Shag rugs and mats are uncommon today.

only two colors be used in bed coverings. Coverlets were loomed in geometric patterns similar to those of the World and also conformed to the two-hue rule, though color gradations (reds shading to pinks) created some interesting patterns.

Distinguishing these bed coverings from worldly examples is made less difficult by the fact that Shaker pieces were marked with embroidered initials in order to identify those assigned to a particular member of the building in which they were used. For example, *R. B.* indicated Sister Rebecca Burris while *S* identified the South Family; the addition of a number indicated which room the piece belonged in.

RUGS

Shaker practicality dictated the use of floor coverings, which both protected the wooden surfaces and kept them warmer in winter. From the 1830s (when such fabrics first became common in this country) the Shakers made braided, hooked, woven, and knit rugs of several types. The Millennial Laws, other than for a ban on figural designs, were largely silent on rug pattern and color, allowing for great freedom of choice in composition. As a result Shaker rugs are among the brightest and most appealing of community textiles.

ABOVE: A Sisters' bedroom or "retiring room" at Hancock Shaker Village, Massachusetts, with the traditional single beds, a washstand, and a Shaker-made iron stove.

Among the most common of Shaker rugs are those woven or braided from the fabric scraps and worn-out clothing produced in quantity within communities which both manufactured textiles and used them up in short order. As early as 1832 the Watervliet Shakers were making large rag carpets, and rugs and hall runners (some 80 feet long) were produced throughout the northeastern settlements from New York to Maine. (In Sabbathday Lake, they were still being made in the 1980s.) Woven on large looms, these floor coverings differed from similar worldly examples in an overall design concept that featured narrow strips of brightly colored (red, green, blue, purple, rose, and black were common), often diagonally striped fabric, set in a repeating pattern, and bound or edged by thick braid or tape.

Consistency in design was encouraged by the Millennial Laws, which dictated that "the carpets in one room should be as near alike as can be provided." Interestingly enough, strictures also mandated how members should traverse community stairs and halls in order to avoid fraying the carpeting: "They should not slip their feet on the carpet, or floor, but lift them up and set them down plumb, so as not to wear out the carpets."

Shaker hand-braided rugs were also made of rags or strips of cloth, though here the fabric was sewn together end to end in a long strand which was then braided and bound around and around in a circular or oval shape. Many similar rugs and mats were, and are today, made in worldly homes; as with their woven rugs, however, the Shakers showed a preference for distinct patterns featuring con-

BELOW: Knit and braided rag mat, c. 1900–1930; dyed silk and rayon, New York or Massachusetts. Small mats like this were used on chairs or the tops of tables.

centric rings of color, often with black or navy borders. Unusual forms like the lobed or scalloped examples from Hancock may also be found. Larger throw rugs in wool and cotton were made for community use, while small place or chair mats of brightly colored braided velvets were produced for sale at the Trustees' stores.

Waste fabric was also used to produce hooked rugs. These generally small pieces were made by drawing strips of fabric through a burlap backing to create a raised or pile surface. During the Victorian era many such rugs were produced within the northeastern settlements, apparently only for community use. Remaining examples show floral and geometric designs typical of the period; however, they are distinguished by braided borders, a detail rarely found in worldly hooked rugs.

LEFT: Penny rug, c. 1890–1910; felt, New York or New England. Made by sewing together fabric discs, these floor coverings were often produced by children.

Similar in appearance to hooked rugs but differently constructed were shirred rugs, which were made by folding fabric strips in half, then running a thread through them, and drawing them up into ruffled or shirred clusters called "caterpillars." These were then sewn to a heavy cloth backing.

The Believers at Pleasant Hill, Kentucky, produced many shirred rugs, including some charming folksy examples featuring horses, an unusual choice of subject matter considering the customary prohibition on the use of pictorial designs. Most examples, however, are in floral or geometric patterns and have the braided borders characteristic of Shaker hooked rugs. The majority of Kentucky shirred rugs are thought to date from about 1840 to 1870, earlier than the hooked examples from the northeast.

Yet another type of rug was the dollar mat or scaled rug. Using a punch-like tool, Shaker Sisters would cut silver dollar–size circles from several layers of fabric. These would then be folded in quarters and sewn in tight clusters to a backing, giving the effect of a high pile. Variations in color and arrangement allowed for interesting floral and geometric patterns. A simpler version in which the circles were overlapped and sewn down flat is thought by some to have been made by community children. Many dollar mats too had the customary Shaker braided border. Though there are examples from other settlements, most dollar mats were made at

BELOW: A patented loom for the weaving of rag rugs used at South Union, Kentucky. The Shakers produced a variety of hooked and woven floor coverings both for their own use and for worldly sale.

ABOVE: Braided rag rug with scalloped border, c. 1850–1880; wool and cotton dyed in various colors, Hancock Shaker Village, Massachusetts. The bold colors and careful design are typical features of Shaker rugs.

Pleasant Hill. Similar pieces were made in the World, but these employ fabric circles of various sizes, while Shaker ones were always of uniform diameter.

The Shakers also turned out many round soft-knitted and crocheted rugs. In the former, yarn was knitted into long tubes which were then stitched together in a spiraling circle. In the latter, the material employed was rag but the effect was the same, a floor covering or mat which, with its alternating bands of darker and lighter hues, looked very much like a braided rug.

Another common type of rug, now rather frequently encountered by collectors, is the shag mat. This was made by folding over one-inch by six-inch strips of cloth and then pulling them through a loose knitted or crocheted backing to create a high, ragged pile. Unlike most Shaker floor coverings, shag rugs usually lack a definite pattern, having at most several concentric rectangles in contrasting hues.

SAMPLERS

The rarest and most costly of Shaker-made textiles are samplers. Like worldly examples, these are characterized by alphabets and numerals done in a variety of stitches and designed to illustrate a young woman's needlework skills. Among the Shakers, sampler-making was probably encouraged to assure facility in marking initials and numbers on the vast quantities of community bedding and clothing. Shaker samplers appear to be uncommon. Less than fifty have been identified, the largest collection existing at Sabbathday Lake.

Unlike worldly specimens which often feature flowers and pictorial elements, Believers' samplers are customarily quite plain, confined as they are to letters and numbers, though most are dated and bear the maker's name, an exception to the proscription against signing one's work.

Among the more unusual examples is an 1845 Union Village, Ohio, sampler listing the initials of both important figures in the establishment of the faith and the presiding Eldresses at the time

RIGHT: Needlework sampler, c. 1840–1850, by Betty Crosman, a Shaker Sister. Unlike worldly examples, Shaker samplers tend to be very plain and undecorated.

the piece was created; and a rare example has been discovered embellished with a house, possibly a Shaker dwelling. The latter piece, which sold at auction in 1992 for $4,000, was made in 1860, by which time the Millennial Laws had been considerably relaxed.

CLOTHING

Shaker clothing displayed, at least until the late nineteenth century, an institutional quality. Millennial strictures against personal adornment as well as a constant concern that no Believer's appearance excite the envy of others combined to assure uniformity in both women's and men's wear. In addition, since the sect maintained—with minor practical changes—the costume worn when the first Believers were "gathered" in the late eighteenth century, their garb appeared distinctly old-fashioned.

This did not mean, however, that members had few clothes. In fact, they had a greater variety than many of their neighbors. Different status and different jobs required different clothing. Young girls, not yet of age for admission to the order, dressed differently than adult Sisters. Everyday dress differed from "meeting dress," and a particular task might require a certain type of clothing, such as the striped black-and-tan dresses and brown-and-white aprons worn by the kitchen crew at Mount Lebanon. Small wonder that Shaker communities had so many cupboards and drawers.

In fact, the Shaker Elders were concerned about this superfluity of costume. In their *Circular Concerning the Dress of Believers*, issued in 1866, the Mount Lebanon ministry lamented: "It is believed that few people on earth in proportion to their numbers spend so much for dress, as do the Shakers; few have so many suits, and such a variety of clothing on hand at once, belonging to the individual! Often times several changes to the season that are supernumerary!"

Examples of this clothing may be seen at several museums and restorations, including Hancock Shaker Village, Shakertown at Pleasant Hill, and the Shaker Museum at Old Chatham, New York; however, relatively few pieces will be found in private collections due both to difficulty in identifying authentic clothing and relatively little collector interest in such items.

BELOW: Reenactor working at a Shaker loom owned by Shakertown, Pleasant Hill, Kentucky. Kentucky Shakers produced a variety of woven fabrics in everything from wool to silk.

LEFT: Summer bonnet, c. 1880–1910; woven straw lined with padded satin lining and decorated with satin ribbons, New York or New England. Such head coverings were both worn by Shakers and sold to the World.

There are, however, notable exceptions. One is the so-called Dorothy Cloak, a long cloak with shoulder cape and attached hood which was designed around 1890 by Eldress Dorothy Durgin of Canterbury, New Hampshire. Often custom made, these capes became extremely popular with fashionable women of the world, described in advertisements as "a serviceable and unique wrap . . . for auto, street, or ocean travel." Made of woolen broadcloth, Dorothy Cloaks came in red, blue, gray, green, white, and black. They were made in baby and child sizes as well as for adults. In 1893, Mrs. Grover Cleveland ordered one to wear at her husband's second presidential inauguration.

By 1900, the cloak business was centered at Mount Lebanon, and another Eldress, Emma J. Neal, obtained in the following year a design patent for her version of the cloak. Fashion changes brought the cloak-making business to an end in 1929, but examples that come on the market are snapped up by collectors. A specimen in

BELOW: Unusual cherry sewing table with gallery top, c. 1850–1860; Kentucky.

purple sold for over $1,900 at an auction in 1988. It should also be noted that non-Shaker versions of these cloaks have been produced. These lack the Shaker-made fabric label sewn into authentic cloaks.

Another article of Shaker dress, less common but much sought after, is the silk scarf or kerchief. The South Union, Kentucky, Community began to grow silkworms in 1822, and the production of silk and silk products was carried on there and in Ohio for some years. Woven silk kerchiefs in iridescent colors were worn as shawls or bodice coverings by Shaker Sisters. They were also sold

BELOW: Three women dressed in clothing typical of nineteenth-century Shaker communities. Bonnets were customary with all types of dress, as the head was rarely left uncovered.

LEFT: Building interior, Canterbury Shaker Village, New Hampshire, with a typical Shaker sewing desk and ladder-back side chair. A bent-wood sewing carrier is atop the desk.

LEFT: Reenactor carding wool in the Shaker manner while surrounded by baskets, a wool wheel, and two so-called "walking wheels." Weaving and the making of wool and cotton fabrics were extremely important in communities that attempted to clothe themselves without recourse to worldly fabrics.

LEFT: A small nineteenth-century flax wheel from South Union, Kentucky. Initially, most Shaker communities made their own thread and fabric.

FOLLOWING PAGE: The cloak room in the 1830 dwelling house at Hancock Shaker Village, Massachusetts, showing a nineteenth-century tailoring counter and several Shaker cloaks.

to the World. An example in two shades of purple sold for $2,000 at a 1991 auction, while an extremely rare tie-dyed kerchief sold at the same time for $4,400. Men's silk neckerchiefs or collars were also made at South Union. Each Brother in the community was given one on New Year's Day, 1833.

Shaker knit goods such as mittens, hose, and especially sweaters are also desirable. Most examples cannot be readily distinguished from worldly products, however sweaters often bore a cloth label reading:

Shaker Sweater

Genuine

Hart & Shepard—"Shakers" E. Canterbury, N.H.

"Look for the label" is always good advice for Shaker collectors.

LEFT: Spool holder, c. 1860–1890; ash with maple spools and iron rods, New York or New England. Needlework utensils were a common item among Shaker productions.

LEFT: Doll, c. 1920–1950; composition doll (probably European), dressed in poplar ware cap, woolen cloak, leather shoes, and rayon dress, Maine. Such dolls were among the most popular Shaker souvenirs.

POPLAR WARE: A CURIOUS FABRIC

As the twentieth century advanced and the number of faithful dwindled, the Shakers came to rely more and more on the income generated by their sales of "fancy goods." By far the most popular of these tourist items were poplar ware boxes, a unique and diversified creation. Produced in New York, New Hampshire, and to a very late date in Maine, these small containers included boxes in various shapes—oblong, hexagonal, octagonal, square, round, and rectangular—to be used for storing handkerchiefs, veils, ribbons, studs, sewing materials, cuffs and collars, razors, and other items.

These fragile vessels were produced from poplar cloth, a material woven from the wood of the otherwise generally useless poplar tree. During winter, when the trees were frozen, they were cut and sectioned into two-foot lengths, which were then sliced into very thin but wide strips with a plane the Shakers had designed for the purpose. These strips were next split into 1/8-inch wide bands and finally woven on special looms into a delicate cloth-like material, the warp of which was a white cotton thread. A Shaker journal entry from Sabbathday Lake, Maine, notes that on April 2, 1878, "The Sisters christen their new Loom for weaving the Popple [sic.] Webbing for sale work by putting on a web of one hundred yards warp."

In the weaving process other materials such as sweet grass or oat straw, often dyed to create color contrasts, might be added. In order to strengthen the fabric and prevent raveling, it was cus-

RIGHT: Poplar ware sewing box, c. 1920–1950; poplar cloth with pink satin, cotton backing, and white kid bindings, stenciled mark of the Sabbathday Lake, Maine, Community on the bottom.

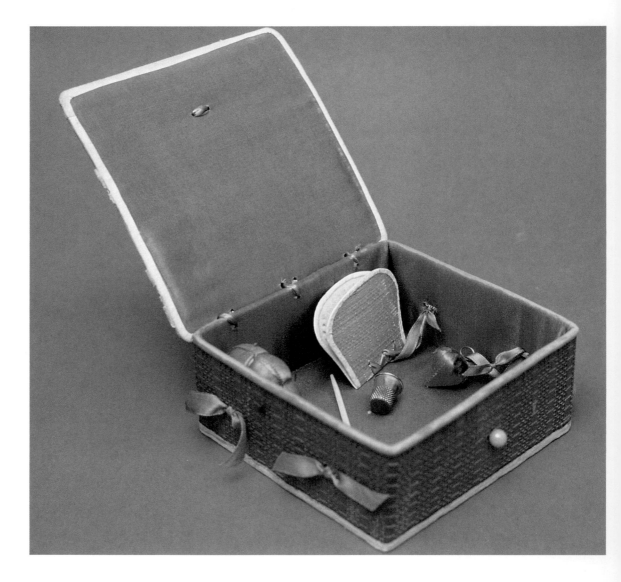

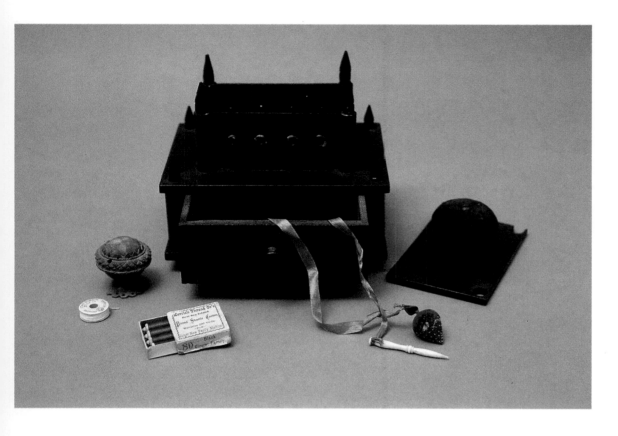

LEFT: Sewing box with accessories, c. 1890–1920; painted pine with ivory, boxwood, and fabric, New York or New England. This late tourist item shows the influence of the Empire style on Shaker design.

BELOW: Armchair with taped seat, c. 1860–1880; maple with woven textile tape, Mount Lebanon, New York. Production chairs like this often bore a decal indicating they were Shaker-made as well as an impressed size number.

tomarily backed with white paper or a fine cotton cloth of the same hue. It was then ready to be used. Finished rolls of the "fabric" were cut with scissors or a paper cutter into the various shapes required for box-making.

There were literally dozens of different box forms, some of which were quite complex, such as the rare bifoid and quatrefoid vessels which consisted of joined semicircular, lidded containers, and the "work caskets," which were larger boxes containing smaller ones within or attached to the exterior surface.

Whatever the form, poplar boxes were all made in much the same manner. The fabric was cut to fit a given pattern, then glued to a matching cardboard backing. The interior was padded and covered with satin (usually pink or white in color), and the vessel was tacked onto a precut pine or poplar base, which was then usually covered with printed paper or wallpaper. As a final touch the seams were bound over with white kid leather. Around 1900, it became customary to ink-stamp the bottom of each piece with the name of the community of origin. Most common today are pieces bearing the Sabbathday Lake mark.

Work or sewing boxes were customarily fitted out with various accessories such as emeries, beeswax, pin and needle folders, scissors, and pincushions. These were attached to the box with pink satin ribbons which were joined in bows on the exterior of the vessel. Other boxes, such as those for gloves, jewelry, and handkerchiefs, were covered with purely decorative bows. All in all, these boxes were, by earlier Shaker standards, shockingly decorative. Circumstances, naturally, alter cases, and these fragile, ornate pieces found

BELOW: Rocking chair with taped back and seat, c. 1880–1910; birch with woven textile tape, Mount Lebanon, New York. Tape seats, developed by the Shakers, were easier to weave and more durable than those made of natural materials.

ready acceptance in the World. Thousands were made, and thousands exist today, many resting as yet undiscovered in work baskets and closets throughout the United States.

Indeed, until recently there was little collector interest in poplar ware. A few dealers handled it, but abundance and its sharp dissimilarity to more highly-prized and much more severe community products like furniture, baskets, and woodenware kept prices low. Then, in 1989, three rare forms appeared at auction. The first, a miniature sewing desk with drawer sold for $2,750. The second form, an oblong double-handled basket with multiple accessories reached $2,400; the last, a tiny heart-shaped box topped by a pincushion, brought an astonishing $2,860. While not triggering great increases in the value of more common forms, which customarily sell in the $100–$500 range, these prices indicated clearly that Shaker poplar ware now had become highly collectible.

However, not all that appears to be poplar ware actually is poplar. By the 1940s most poplar trees on community lands had been cut, making it necessary for the Sisters to substitute a commercially manufactured wallpaper or fabric which they termed "tapestry cloth." Pieces made from this material are considered less desirable, and the collector should always examine closely the composition of any prospective purchase.

It should also be mentioned that the Shakers employed the poplar fabric for other purposes. Chief among these was the manufacture of unbacked place mats, which were sold in the Maine communities' Trustee shops. Made to be discarded, however, these mats are seldom seen today.

RIGHT: View of a building located on the grounds at Shakertown, Pleasant Hill, Kentucky. The well-made fence and orderly grounds reflect the Shakers' respect for the environment.

FRESH
AND
GENUINE
FOR
SALE
HERE.

TE FOR IT

Chapter Five

SHAKER ART AND EPHEMERA

In the course of their long history, the Shakers have left behind a voluminous paper trail, everything from journals and letters to advertising materials connected with their various businesses. All of it is of interest to collectors.

PAPER LABELS

One of the earliest community industries was garden seed propagation. Begun in 1789 at Watervliet, the raising of seeds for sale to the World continued there and at Hancock, Massachusetts, and Enfield, New Hampshire, until after 1850, and at Mount Lebanon to the turn of the century.

Shaker-built label presses turned out a variety of gummed labels for use on seed packets and the larger wooden boxes in which bulk seeds were shipped, and these as well as scarce catalogs are much sought after. The communities also issued gardeners' manuals which both advised the grower as to proper planting methods and promoted Shaker seeds. Even the smallest of these labels can bring high prices. A single framed bean seed label brought $275 at auction in 1989, while a group of five for cayenne pepper sold for over $300; a wooden box labeled *Shaker Seed Co.* reached $1,540.

Probably the most sought after Shaker labels are the decals used to identify chairs sold to the World. Featuring an image of a rocking chair, these were affixed to Shaker products during the 1875–1942 period. A complete set of fifty-five labels for chairs ranging in size from #0 to #7 reached the astounding 1988 auction price of $5,500.

Labels from many other products may be found. The Shakers manufactured a variety of wines, including white currant, apple,

LEFT: A lithographed paper seed box label from Mount Lebanon, New York, dating to the late 1800s. Advertising and colorful labels made Shaker seeds big sellers.

and elderberry as well as apple sauce, dried sweet corn, candied walnuts, and maple sugar cakes, the latter shaped in community-made fluted tin molds. All these products were packaged in colorful paper or cardboard containers, existent examples of which are highly popular with collectors.

Closely related was the business in medicinal herbs. The Shakers avoided worldly doctors, the Millennial Laws of 1845 noting, "the order of God forbids that Believers should employ Doctors of the World, except in some extreme cases, or the case of a sick child, whose parents are among the World, and desire such aid; and in such cases, the Ministry or Elders should decide whether it be proper or not."

Members treated their illnesses with botanical medicine, employing various herbs and roots (many of which were then also utilized by worldly doctors). This too grew into a business. Bottles (not Shaker-made) were labeled with such colorful names as "fleabane," "foxglove," and "pennyroyal," and offered to a grateful public that included doctors and pharmacists. Most of these patent medicines were not harmful and some were even beneficial; however, a few, such as Tincture of Opium, offered at best dubious remedies.

The medicinal herb business generated numerous collectibles: bottles, with the embossed name of the product (such as "Mother Siegel's Laxative Syrup"), labels, advertising materials such as posters, invoices, and the Shaker Almanacs, which combined recipes, weather predictions, house-

BELOW: A group of late nineteenth-century lithographed paper and wood seed boxes from the Mount Lebanon, New York, Community. Shaker seeds were sold throughout the United States.

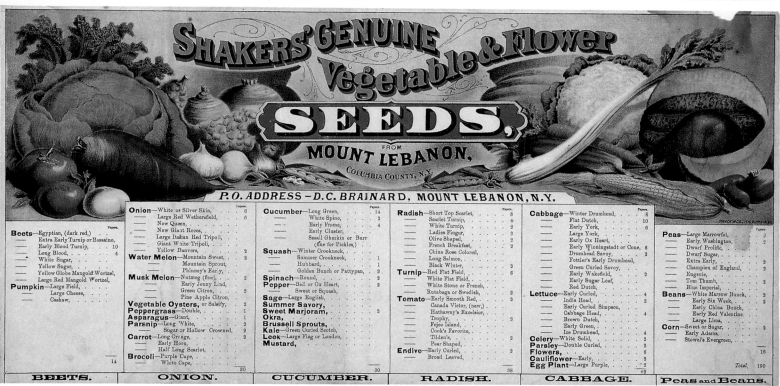

hold hints, and, of course, testimonials to the virtues of community remedies. In the latter the authors seemed often to depart from the sect's traditional modesty, declaring in one case that: "Everything made by the Shakers is good beyond a doubt. Their character stands very high. Everything that the Shakers make sells readily, and always gives satisfaction. When the Shakers put their name on an article you can rely on it."

ABOVE: This advertisement by the Mount Lebanon Community offers a wide variety of vegetables seeds for sale, including numerous types of onions, musk melons, cabbages, and squash.

CATALOGING

Not all Shaker advertisements extolled the virtues of medicines or edibles. There were detailed catalogs covering the famous Shaker cloak, "a unique and comfortable garment," oval boxes, "a combination of neatness and utility," basketry, brooms, and, of course, the renowned Shaker chairs. The first such publication was issued in 1874, and the first dated example a year later; the most well-known appeared in 1876 when Shaker seating was exhibited at the Philadelphia Centennial Exposition. That year's catalog featured views of Exposition buildings as well as Shaker hymns and missionary messages to the World. The latter had little effect but the chairs sold well.

OTHER PAPER EPHEMERA

Ephemera of the sort described above is both popular and relatively common. Much more difficult to obtain is material such as music and sermons prepared for use within the community. In

1990 two important documents—a ten-page manuscript copy of *A Communication from the Prophet Daniel* and the ninety-two-page *Lecture at Enfield*—appeared at auction. The first sold for $2,750; the second for $3,850. Both were handwritten and appeared to date from the mid-nineteenth century, a time of great spiritual activity in the sect.

Among the "gifts" received by Believers during the religious ferment of the 1830–1850 period were numerous songs or hymns, many of which were transcribed for community use in the unique system of musical notation devised by the Shakers. A manuscript song book of this sort, dating to the 1840s, was sold in 1994 for over $6,000. Hymn books, like sermons and other community documents, may often not be recognized by the average collector since the word "Shaker" or other obvious identifying characteristics may be absent. Only a close reading will reveal their origin.

Another important area of Shaker ephemera includes items such as postcards and books which, though often not produced by Shakers, pertained to them. Visitors to the various communities often purchased postcards depicting Shaker buildings or the activities of the sect. In 1911, the Trustees' store at Enfield,

ABOVE: View of the brick dwelling house, erected in 1830, at Hancock Shaker Village, Massachusetts. Though most early Shaker structures were made of wood, by the 1830s the communities, especially in the South and Midwest, were building in brick.

RIGHT: Infirmary area at Hancock Shaker Village, Massachusetts. The unusual adult-size rocking cradles were designed to comfort elderly and infirm patients and are unique to the Shakers.

Connecticut, sold some 1,400 of these. Once sold for a penny (postage was a cent more), these missives now bring $30–$40 apiece. Most sought after are those depicting Shaker Brothers. Women appear more often, possibly because after 1900 they made up the majority of the population.

Curiosity about the Shaker way of life led to numerous books on the sect, the great majority of which were by non-Believers. A rare exception is *The Aletheia. Spirit of Truth*, written in 1907 by Sister Aurelia C. Mace of Sabbathday Lake, Maine. Mace's book, consisting of a series of articles on everything from Shaker beliefs to Shaker cooking, is a highly desirable acquisition. However, many books on Shaker life are collectible, the earliest published being the most desirable.

HEAVENLY IMAGES

The idea of art seems contradictory in a society whose members were forbidden to display paintings, prints, or other artwork and were constantly cautioned against any sort of personal expression that, in the words of the Millennial Laws, "will have a tendency to feed pride and vanity." Nevertheless, the Shaker communities did produce artworks, including a small group of extraordinary watercolor folk paintings.

Early Shaker belief was substantially mystical in content, with members following Mother Ann Lee's direction in patterning their lives on what they perceived to be direct revelations or commands from God. While this element was always important in the faith it reached a high point during the 1830–1850 revival period when numerous Believers professed to have received such messages. In his journal for the year 1840, Brother Isaac Newton Youngs of Mount Lebanon noted that "there was an abundance of readings, of various gifts, visions, messages, etc., etc. And new songs in profusion, mostly through inspiration and a good portion of them by those who were no natural singers."

FAR LEFT: Lithographed paper label for Shaker Tamar Laxative, one of many popular community remedies. The medicine was prepared at the Sabbathday Lake, Maine, Community.

LEFT: Interior of an infirmary, showing various herbal remedies, medicine bottles, and carriers. The Shakers developed numerous cures and were quite advanced in their treatment of the ill and aged.

FOLLOWING PAGE:
Buildings at Hancock Shaker Village, Massachusetts. The architectural variations reflect changing styles over a long period of occupation.

Faith   Hope   Honesty   Continence   Innocence   Simplicity   Meekness   Humility   Prudence   Patience

INSPIRATIONAL DRAWINGS

Noteworthy among these "gifts" are a group of ink and watercolor drawings on paper done during this time by various Shaker Sisters and referred to by writers in the field as "spirit" or "inspirational" drawings, or simply as "spiritual gifts." It is likely that several hundred of these were produced, but only about sixty remain today, mostly in public collections such as those at Hancock Shaker Village and The Western Reserve Historical Society. A circular drawing featuring a variety of birds and flowers and inscribed "words of Holy Mother . . . Wisdom to Sally Lomise, May 20th 1847" was sold at auction in August, 1990, bringing the somewhat astounding price of $49,500. Another example had been purchased in 1983 for over $8,000.

Inspirational drawings typically combine various figurative elements with handwritten text, expressions of faith, a message of endearment to another member of the community, a brief song, or a claimed revelation from Mother Ann or another of the sect's early leaders. They are often dated and sometimes signed. Since both the pictorial elements and the signatures violated community standards

LEFT: Spirit or inspirational drawing, *City of Pease* [sic.], c. 1835–1845; water color on paper, New York or New England. Most of such work was created by Shaker Sisters with no particular artistic training.

BELOW: Spirit or inspirational drawing, *A Golden Crown of Comford and Rest*, c. 1840–1850; water color on paper, New York or New England. Flowers similar to the ones seen here appear in worldly theorem paintings of the same period.

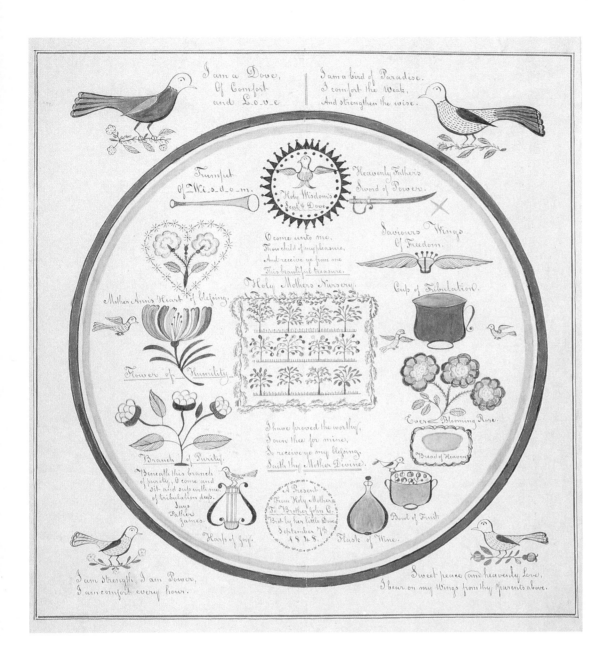

ABOVE: Spirit or inspirational drawing, *A Gift From Holy Mother Wisdom To Brother John C.*, dated 1848; water color on paper, New York or New England. These paintings were believed by their creators to be divinely inspired.

of the period, it has been assumed that these "gifts" were indeed gifts, intended for private rather than communal distribution.

Religious motivation notwithstanding, it would appear that these works come directly out of the early nineteenth-century tradition of love tokens, the forerunner of the modern-day valentine. The combination of calligraphy with symbols of affections, such as the heart and dove, suggests that even in a society where personal feelings were strongly suppressed, affection would find a way, even if couched in the most oblique religious language.

Most drawings are symmetrical in design with elaboration in patterning, progressing over time from simple geometric shapes in the mid-1830s to the leaves, hearts, and fans of the 1840s, and toward the complex imagery of the 1850 period.

Musical elements are an important distinguishing characteristic, reflecting the role that music took in Shaker religious observances. Musical instruments such as the harp and trumpet with a biblical connotation appear frequently, while musical notation is sometimes used as a design element. Expressions of faith may be masked in musical terminology, as in:

I have a little drum the Mother gave to me
The prettiest little drum that ever you did see
I'll drum night and day, I'll drum night and day
To call volunteers to fight sin away.

While some artists, such as Sister Hannah Cahoon of Mount Lebanon, claimed that they had been directed in their work by angels, it appears to me that the inspiration for these drawings was more a worldly one, and the Shakers, as was their way, simply modified and distilled a form of contemporary folk art to achieve their own unique interpretation.

Maps and Plans

Practical as well as spiritual needs brought deviation from the Millennial rules against decorative paintings and drawings. As the Believers' communities expanded it became necessary to document their growth and holdings. Village plans and maps of land acquisitions were required. One of the most prolific authors of such drawings was Elder Joshua Bussell (1816–1900) of the Alfred, Maine, settlement. Some seventeen drawings of the community, many signed, have been attributed to him. The earliest, dating to the mid-1840s, are simply maps. By the 1870s, though, his drawings reflected a knowledge of perspective and a desire to add elements, such as animals, vehicles, and pedestrians; while not necessary to the purpose of his work they did reflect an artistic impulse.

Another well-known Shaker map- and plan-maker was Elder Henry Clay Blinn (1824–1905) of Canterbury. His highly detailed "Plan of Canterbury, New Hampshire," done in ink and watercolor on paper, preserves a detailed view of a community that has now largely vanished. The efforts of Bussell and Blinn notwithstanding, it appears that relatively few Shaker maps and settlement plans were made and fewer yet have survived. They seldom appear on the market.

BELOW: Spirit or inspirational drawing, *Holy Mother Wisdom To Daniel Boler*, dated 1847; water color on paper, New York or New England. Like most such works, this one may have reflected the artist's knowledge of contemporary love tokens or valentines.

ABOVE: *The Round Barn*, Hancock Shaker Village, Massachusetts, 1985. Contemporary folk artist Kathy Jakobsen has painted several Shaker views, including this one of the famous barn at Hancock.

RIGHT: Residents of nearby communities dressed in Shaker clothing gather at a meetinghouse in Shaker Village, Pleasantville, Kentucky.

FOLK PAINTINGS

By the twentieth century, many of the Millennial strictures, including those that inhibited art, had fallen into disuse. Moreover, the remaining communities, whose population more and more consisted primarily of older women unable to run the farm or shops, looked for other sources of income.

Among the items that sold well in Trustees' shops were postcards, and Sister C. H. Sarle (d. 1955) of the Canterbury, New Hampshire, Community added to the lithographed or photographed views of Shakers and Shaker dwellings her own detailed oils-on-cardboard paintings of village scenes. Postcard-size, and intended to be sold in competition with them, these charming miniature views were usually signed or initialed by the artist. The Sister also painted similar scenes in oils on the tops of round Shaker boxes.

Though she did not begin to paint until late in life, Sister Sarle was a natural and prolific artist, turning out hundreds of works, most of which remain to be discovered by the growing number of avid and passionate collectors of Shaker-made arts and crafts.

INDEX

Lakes and fjords are "the mirror of Norway." The reflection of mountain and forest on the surface of a lake multiplies the beauty of a pastoral scene. In a time gone by, the clear, haunting sound of the *lur*—a long, wooden shepherd's horn—floated over the valley and echoed from surrounding hillsides as it carried a message to neighbor or friend.